Autonomous and Self-Directed Learning: Agentic Perspectives

Michael K. Ponton and Paul B. Carr
Editors

WATERTREE PRESS

Autonomous and Self-Directed Learning
Agentic Perspectives

Published by Watertree Press, LLC
PO Box 16763, Chesapeake, VA 23328
http://www.watertreepress.com

Notice of Liability

The information in this book is distributed on an "as is" basis, without warranty. While every precaution has been taken in the preparation of this book, the publisher and authors make no claim or guarantee as to its correctness, usefulness, or completeness for any reason, under any circumstance. Moreover, the publisher and authors shall have no liability to any person or entity with respect to loss or damages caused or alleged to have been caused directly or indirectly by the information contained in this book.

Publisher's Cataloging-in-Publication Data

Names: Ponton, Michael K. | Carr, Paul B.

Title: Autonomous and Self-Directed Learning: Agentic Perspectives

Description: Chesapeake, VA: Watertree Press LLC, 2016

Identifiers: ISBN: 978-0-9911046-6-6 (pbk.)

Subjects: LCSH: Adult learning. | Adult education. | Adult education–
  Research. BISAC: EDUCATION / Adult & Continuing Education. |
  EDUCATION / Research. | EDUCATION / Teaching Methods & Materials
  / General.

Classification: LCC LC5215 | DDC 374–dc22

Printed in the United States of America

CONTENTS

Preface

Part I: Theoretical Discussions

Part II: Research Findings

Part III: Instrumentation Issues

Notes:
[1]Reprint permission not required.
[2]Copyright held by publisher; reprinted with permission.

PREFACE

For nearly two decades, we have formulated discussions of self-directed and autonomous learning by building upon the conceptual frameworks provided by Professors Emeriti Gary Confessore (learner autonomy and conation) and Albert Bandura (social cognitive theory, human agency, and self-efficacy). Using an agentic perspective of personal agency to describe learning, the agent as a learner engages in forethought to adopt goals of personal value and formulate learning plans; reacts to this ideation by enacting plans; reflects upon consequences and outcomes; and uses this acquired information to inform future learning plans. Our work and that with our colleagues has included both theoretical discussions and original research. This edited compendium, primarily consisting of previously published articles, is the result of these efforts.

Despite editing, each chapter is consistent with the content of its original form; therefore, topic redundancies are included that serve to reinforce essential concepts and perspectives. Note that only those articles deemed essential in providing salient aspects of our conceptualizations of self-directed and, more generally, autonomous learning are presented. Our intent is that this compendium will represent a convenient resource for understanding not only our current thinking but also its historical development.

As coauthors for included articles, we thank Professors Gary Confessore, Gail Derrick, Michael Hall, Nancy Rhea Wiggers, and Christine Schuette for their scholarly contributions and willingness to include their work as chapters. We have supported each other in our personal and intellectual lives for many years now and hope to continue our collaboration in extending the discussion of human agency in learning.

Professor Ponton acknowledges Regent University for providing a sabbatical that afforded an opportunity to think and work on this compendium.

Michael K. Ponton and Paul B. Carr, Editors
Professors of Education
Regent University
Virginia Beach, VA

CHAPTER 1

A QUASI-LINEAR BEHAVIORAL MODEL AND AN APPLICATION TO SELF-DIRECTED LEARNING[1]

A model is presented that describes the relationship between one's knowledge of the world and the concomitant personal behaviors that serve as a mechanism to obtain desired outcomes. Integrated within this model are the differing roles that outcomes serve as motivators and as modifiers to one's worldview. The model is dichotomized between general and contextual applications. Because learner self-directedness (a personal characteristic) involves cognition and affection while self-directed learning (a pedagogic process) encompasses conation, behavior, and introspection, the model can be dichotomized again in another direction. Presented also are the roles that cognitive motivation theories play in moving an individual through this behavioral model and the roles of wishes, self-efficacy, opportunity, and self-influence.

Frese (1997) stated that *dynamic self-reliance* is increasing in value as a personal characteristic necessary for success in the jobs of the next century. The critical components of dynamic self-reliance are the ability "to acquire knowledge and skills by oneself (self-training) and to self-start motivational processes (initiative)" (p. 399). Frese asserted that personal initiative is "the centerpiece of self-reliance" (p. 408) and is the behavior in which people "do not wait for orders, suggestions or ideas from other people, but develop their own ideas and start acting themselves" (pp. 408-409). This behavior occurs even at the risk of taking on additional, self-generated tasks. Although Frese opined the importance of self-training and initiative for occupational success, their conjoint relationship is inherent to the activity of self-directed learning.

Learning can be defined as "acquiring knowledge and skills as the result of experience" (Popplestone & McPherson, 1988, p. 212). Hiemstra (1994) asserted a characteristic of self-directed learning is that the individual learner may become empowered with an increasing

---

[1]NASA Technical Memorandum 209094 (1999)

responsibility for making decisions associated with the learning endeavor. In other words, the learner (i.e., self) is responsible for directing the creation of the experiences that provide knowledge and skills for acquisition (i.e., learning). Covey (1989) stated that initiative "mean[s] recognizing our responsibility to make things happen" (p. 75) which, for a self-directed learner, would be the creation of the learning event itself (Ponton & Confessore, 1998). Tough (1982) conservatively estimated that approximately 80% of adult learners conduct learning under their own volition thus accenting the importance for studying self-directed learning.

Self-directed learning is also important in the area of leadership. Vaill (1996) defined leadership as the initiative to perform self-directed learning. He asserted that before a leader issues a directive, he or she must take the "initiative . . . [in] thinking through (learning) what is needed and why" (p. 134). This autonomous learning instills conviction in the leader as to what is the appropriate course of action. An important responsibility of the leader is to lead the followers through this learning process so that they too will understand the rationale of the decision and subsequently support the action (Vaill, 1996). This exercise is critical in the development of future leaders (Ponton & Confessore, 1998).

The definition of self-directed learning can vary subtly or considerably from one researcher to another thereby representing a major concern among scholars in this field (Oddi, 1987). Long (1998) asserted that the research in self-directed learning can be conceptualized under one of four major paradigms: sociological, teaching technique, methodological, and psychological. Long posited that each paradigm has a requisite set of implications and assumptions. However, he asserted that of these four paradigms, only "the *psychological conceptualization* is both necessary and sufficient to explain SDL [self-directed learning]" (Long, 1998, p. 10). He stated,

> the psychological conceptualization implies that fundamentally learning is a self-initiated, self-directed, and self-regulated cognitive process whereby the learner can choose to ignore instruction, to merely absorb it by casual attention, to carefully memorize without critical reflection, or to seek to change or create an understanding of information. (p. 9)

The purpose of this chapter is to present a perspective of the pedagogic process of self-directed learning by incorporating the mechanisms of self-initiation, self-directedness, and self-regulation into a quasi-linear behavioral model. The proposed model is quasi-linear in that structurally its components (cognition, affection, conation, etc.) appear to be linearly independent. In fact, great interaction occurs between the components via introspection, movement within the model occurs via self-influence, and inputs to the model can occur via processes external to the model itself. Thus, actual behavior is correctly characterized as a nonlinear process where such a process represents an "intricate system of interacting variables" (Volk, 1995, p. 184). Also characteristic of a nonlinear process (and therefore of behavior as well) is that small perturbations in the initial conditions can cause large and sometimes unpredictable changes in the resultant outcome (Baker & Gollub, 1990; Schroeder, 1991). The quasi-linear behavioral model is presented as a tool that may clarify one's perspective of self-directed learning.

Because self-directed learning represents a subset of the behavioral activities that any individual may engage in, presented first is a simple behavioral model in which volitional behavior is predicated on cognition, affection, and conation. Based on this rudimentary understanding, a less simple model will be presented to further explain self-regulatory behavior with an ultimate application to self-directed learning. The influence of self-directed learning to the success of subordinate workers (Frese, 1997), leaders (Vaill, 1996), and learners in general warrants the development of behavioral models that enhance our understanding of this theoretical construct.

A Simple Behavioral Model

Fishbein and Ajzen (1975) provide a general model that indicates the relationship between beliefs, attitudes, behavioral intentions, and behaviors (see Figure 1). Beliefs provide the knowledge base upon which we know the world. Objects of one's beliefs can be a "person, issue, or event" (Fishbein & Ajzen, 1975, p. 12) or even a behavior. Within the cognition of belief formulation, objects are assigned attributes. Using these attributes, one develops an attitude toward the object. Attitude refers to a consistently favorable or unfavorable response to the given object (Fishbein & Ajzen, 1975) and is an affective process.

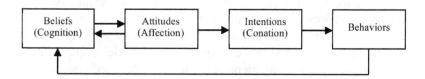

Figure 1. A simple behavioral model (Fishbein & Ajzen, 1975).

For example, one's beliefs may include the following attributive assignments: (a) Corvettes are fast cars, (b) Corvettes are sleek-looking cars, and (c) Corvettes are engineering feats. If one valued fast, sleek-looking, and state-of-the-art-engineered cars, then one would exude a favorable attitude toward Corvettes provided that these were the only attributes under consideration. As Fishbein and Ajzen (1975) asserted, attitudes feed back into beliefs (see Figure 1). Based on this presupposed favorable attitude toward Corvettes, one may look for and assign additional attributes that reinforce this favorable attitude. In addition, attitudes toward specific American-made cars may influence beliefs about American-made cars in general. (Note that another individual may feel unfavorably toward the Corvette because of a lack of value placed on the aforementioned attributes.)

Based on the presumed favorable attitude toward the Corvette, one may then intend to own a Corvette. Intention refers to a determination to engage in an action or to reach a desired future state. A behavioral intention is a determination to perform a particular behavior. Our intention here is ultimate ownership of a Corvette (desired future state). At this point, an acquisition plan must be formulated. For example, should one work extra hours to earn the money needed to purchase a Corvette or should one merely steal one?

As Fishbein and Ajzen (1975) stated, these potential behaviors now become the objects of another pass through the model. Note that the arrows in the model indicate movement but are not restrictively unidirectional; self-reflection occurs at each arrow to provide interpretation for self-regulatory volition of movement within the model. The option of stealing is assigned attributes (cognition) and based on one's feelings toward these attributes one develops an attitude (affection) toward stealing. If the attitude is favorable, then behavioral intentions to steal are developed.

Intentions are highly correlated to behaviors if "intention and behavior correspond in their levels of specificity . . . and the degree to which carrying out the intention is completely under the person's volitional control" (Fishbein & Ajzen, 1975, p. 369). A behavioral intention is referred to as a conation where a conation is "an instinctually motivated biological striving that may appear . . . in behavior as action tendencies" (Gove, 1976, p. 468).

Action theory describes the process in which one acts on the environment and the results of these actions provide feedback that shapes one's worldview.

> The basic premise of action theory is that human beings interpret their own and others' behavior in terms of action-related concepts such as goals, plans, intentions, and beliefs and that their actions are in part determined by those reflexive interpretations. (Chapman & Skinner, 1985, p. 201)

Such introspective interpretations permit an individual's self-regulatory movement within the model. These new beliefs create the foundation upon which the cycle repeats.

Frese and Sabini (1985) stated that wishes actually precede intentions. The difference between wishes and intentions is in the level of correlation to behavior. Wishes require opportunity to become intentions. Until an opportunity is perceived to exist, the wish remains dormant but can be easily aroused when an opportunity presents itself. But to what end are we attempting to reach by engaging in the development of beliefs, attitudes, wishes, intentions, and ultimately performing desired behaviors? That is, where is the motivation?

Bandura (1997) provided insight by presenting the difference between outcomes and performance goals. Expected outcomes represent the results that one truly hopes will be gained by performing selected behaviors. Actual outcomes are the real outcomes that occur. Outcomes can be physical (e.g., pleasure or pain), social (e.g., acceptance, rejection, promotion, or money), or self-evaluative. Self-evaluative outcomes represent a comparison between one's behaviors or the outcomes of one's behaviors and self-standards. Performance goals are differentiated from outcomes in that they have metrics of accomplishment and are the direct result of a performance. For example, an athlete may be motivated to long jump 29 feet (performance goal) in order to gain social acceptance (expected outcome). The athlete is motivated to engage in the behavior because he or she perceives that the correlation between the performance goal and the expected outcome is great. If actual outcomes are different than expected outcomes, then behaviors performed to accomplish the latter may be reevaluated.

Fishbein and Ajzen (1975) stated that attitudes can predict general behaviors but not specific ones. Thus, if one has a favorable attitude toward the personal consumption of bourbon (in comparison to other forms of liquor), then one may, in general, drink bourbon when opportunities arise. However, to state emphatically that this person will drink bourbon on a specified occasion based on his or her bourbon attitude is impossible because of the influence of competing factors. This person may be responsible for driving on a particular occasion whereby the unfavorable attitude toward drinking and driving has priority over the favorable attitude toward drinking bourbon.

Behaviors become hierarchical based on the values assigned to them. According to social cognitive theory, human agency is predicted on the triadic reciprocal interaction between personal behavior, internal personal factors, and the environment where all three determinants interact with various magnitudes of influence dependent upon the context (Bandura, 1997). The personal factors are one's cognitive, biological, and affective characteristics and the environment represents everything external to the individual.

Thus, one's value system affects the model by not only influencing the attitudes toward the attributes and ultimately the objects in one's belief structure but also toward the actual outcomes of behavioral performances (self-evaluation). But if personal values are important, where are they in the model? Also, one does not have an attitude toward everything one knows about. There are many objects that a person "knows" via personal experience or vicarious modeling (cf. Bandura, 1965; Bandura, 1977b) and attributes may be assigned to these objects that could have personal meaning. Yet the person maintains neither a favorable nor unfavorable predisposition toward these objects. How does this model account for this situation? If outcomes are so important because they serve as both the motivation and the feedback of behaviors, then where are they in the model?

A Less Simple Behavioral Model

A proposed model is presented in Figure 2. This model incorporates the presence of outcomes and wishes and is framed to include general and contextual applications.

General Beliefs, Attitudes, and Desired Outcomes

Everything that one knows is categorized under the general belief rubric. Note that *know* does not necessitate factual information. If one assigns completely erroneous attributes to a given object but that person truly believes that the assignments are valid, then these object-attribute assignments are part of the individual's belief structure. Thus, general beliefs provide the foundation upon which everything else is formed. But one does not enter the world with beliefs (i.e., knowledge of the world). It is through action theory that one learns about the world to formulate beliefs. A newborn acts on the world via behaviors that include observational modeling (Bandura, 1977b) and eventually grows to initiate more dynamic interactions and models of increasingly complex behaviors. Through these influential interactions, a person develops beliefs and *knows* the world.

Based on this general belief structure, one then develops general attitudes. In this context, general attitudes refer to one's value system. Based on his or her worldview, one develops favorable or unfavorable attitudes toward many objects that coalesce under a particular value rubric. For example, the multitude of object-attribute assignments that ultimately produce a high value on the preservation of human life is complex and is certainly unique for every person who possesses this value. The complexity arises because values are the result of specific favorable *and* unfavorable attitudes toward many objects and because these attitudes interact with the belief structure itself. Because beliefs are also affected by behaviors and according to social cognitive theory behaviors are influenced by the person and the environment (as well as influencing the person and environment), the development of the value system must be derived from everything the person knows (i.e., the general beliefs).

After the general attitudes (i.e., value system) are developed, personal determinations are made concerning what one is interested in getting out of life based upon what one has determined to be important. This process results in the formulation of general desired outcomes. These desired outcomes form the outcome goals (as differentiated from performance goals) that motivate the person to determine the contextual activities that may lead to the accomplishment of these outcomes. According to goal theory, the disparity that exists between one's current state and one's desired state provides "a major cognitive mechanism of motivation and self-directedness" (Bandura, 1997, p. 128).

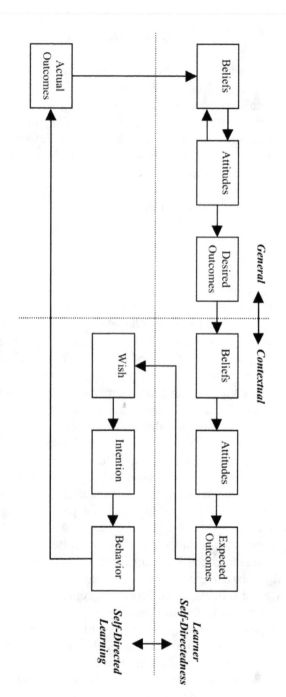

Figure 2. A less simple behavioral model.

At this stage, however, the motivation is general and is not predictive of contextual behavior; that is, there is a motivation to engage in some, as yet unspecified, behavior to accomplish desired outcomes. As an example, the desired outcome of being named the chief scientist of a large research organization (social outcome) would serve as a motivating factor in assessing which behaviors are needed to reach this outcome goal. Such behaviors considered may range from personal development to developing political liaisons or some combination thereof. An additional desired outcome of being competent by one's internal standards (self-evaluative outcome) may lead to the ultimate determination to engage in behaviors that are perceived to help accomplish both desired outcomes.

Contextual Beliefs, Attitude, Expected Outcomes, and Learner Self-Directedness

At this point, the individual begins to focus on specific objects that will lead to his or her desired outcomes. One can now distinguish between two phenomena: learner self-directedness and self-directed learning. Learner self-directedness includes the internal characteristics of a person (cognition and affection) that create the motivation for subsequent behavioral intentions (conations) and behavior. The pedagogic process of self-directed learning includes the behavioral intentions, behaviors, and the subsequent self-reflection; thus, Figure 2 is dichotomized accordingly.

After desired outcomes are determined, one will focus on specific processes—such as self-directed learning—that one may feel will produce performance goals and will support the ultimate accomplishment of these desired outcomes. Whereas many behaviors may support the accomplishment of desired outcomes, this chapter will focus on the process of self-directed learning. For example, consider the illustration mentioned previously concerning the person who desires to become the chief scientist of a large research organization. As already mentioned, this individual may choose to consider behaviors associated with political positioning rather than self-directed learning activities in order to achieve this desired outcome. This decision is largely predicated on the expectation that particular behaviors will lead to valued outcomes, the premise of the expectancy value theory of cognitive motivation (Howard, 1989).

Although one may develop beliefs and an attitude toward self-directed learning in general (the object of general beliefs), this model incorporates the contextual importance of learner self-directedness that leads to the intentional behavior included in self-directed learning. Thus, the object of the belief is contextual in nature. One may apply completely different attributes and develop different attitudes toward the self-directed learning of particle physics as compared to the operation of a new blender. But the attributes that we assign to either situation are based on the general framework of our belief structure.

After beliefs have been formulated about the contextual self-directed learning activity (i.e., the contextual object), attitudes are developed. These attitudes may include self-efficacy assessments. Self-efficacy refers "to beliefs in one's capabilities to organize and execute the courses of action required to produce given attainments" (Bandura, 1997, p. 3). The major information sources of efficacy appraisals are performance accomplishments, vicarious experiences, verbal persuasions, and emotional arousal (Bandura, 1977a). Therefore, one may apply attributes to the contextual self-directed learning activity that one may feel unfavorably toward due to a lack of perceived ability, or vice-versa. This is the feedback process indicated previously between beliefs and attitudes.

After the attitude is formed, an assessment is made concerning the expected outcomes of the self-directed learning; that is, if one decides to engage in a self-directed learning activity to accomplish some desired level of competence (performance goal), then will this performance result lead to outcomes (expected outcomes) that support desired outcomes? Note that this is a cognitive/affective process involving anticipatory considerations. This perceived correlation between performance results and expected outcomes is based on what one believes about the performance thus resulting in a feeling of the magnitude of the correlation. If the magnitude of the correlation is perceived to be high, then the individual creates a wish to engage in the self-directed learning activity.

At this point, an assessment is made concerning the perceived opportunity to engage in the performance. One will not wish to engage in an activity that will hopefully lead to highly valued and highly prioritized outcomes unless one believes that the opportunity is present for such a performance to occur.

Opportunities can be both external and internal in nature. Confessore (1992) asserted that a successful self-directed learning activity is predicated on the presence of the four factors of personal "drive, initiative, resourcefulness and persistence" (p. 3). These factors are foundational to the personal determination of the existence of a self-directed learning opportunity. If, for example, one does not feel self-efficacious in planning a learning activity where planning is a behavior associated with resourcefulness (Rosenbaum, 1989), then the individual may not perceive that an opportunity exists for this learning activity. Or perhaps the individual does not perceive the availability of requisite learning resources. In either case, opportunity is lacking. Without opportunity, other behaviors that are perceived to produce performances that correlate with expected outcomes may subsequently serve as objects for beliefs and affects or the wish to engage in the self-directed learning may wait dormant until facilitative opportunities arise. The time scale is predicated on the hierarchical value attributed to desired outcomes.

If the opportunity to engage in a self-directed learning activity is perceived to exist, then the wish changes to a behavioral intention. Contingent on the presence of sufficient motivational processes, intention/behavior specificity, and personal volition, behavioral intentions transform into behaviors. Such behaviors produce performances with actual outcomes that are interpreted via reflexive self-evaluation. These actual outcomes influence our perceptions (beliefs and affects) of contextual and general objects of consideration (Figure 2).

A summary of the proposed model presented in Figure 2 is as follows. An individual develops an understanding of the world (i.e., general beliefs) and based on this understanding creates a value system (i.e., general attitudes). These values lead to general outcomes that are desired from life. Based on these general desired outcomes, the individual evaluates specific behaviors that may lead to expected outcomes that support these desired outcomes (i.e., contextual beliefs, attitudes, and expected outcomes). If the correlation between behavioral performances and expected outcomes is perceived to be high, then a wish is developed to engage in the behavior (i.e., contextual wish). Based on the presence of opportunity, the contextual wish is transformed into an intention and a subsequent behavior (i.e., contextual intention and behavior). Through self-reflection, the actual outcomes are evaluated and provide input into the model (i.e., general actual outcomes into general beliefs).

Implications to Self-Directed Learning

For self-directed learning to occur, learner self-directedness must be present. This means that the individual must feel that self-directed learning is a viable means to accomplish desired outcomes from life. Thus, self-directed learning becomes the contextual object of belief and attitude.

The individual learns that self-directed learning is an effective approach initially through vicarious modeling and then gains in self-efficacy with successful learning endeavors referred to as mastery experiences (Bandura, 1997). Because successful self-directed learning is predicated on numerous factors that include, for example, personal initiative and resourcefulness (Confessore, 1992), intervention strategies can be formulated to diagnose and reduce weaknesses in a learner's ability to engage in necessary behaviors that lead to success.

As an example, personal initiative is described as a behavior syndrome of co-occurring behaviors (Frese et al., 1996; Frohman, 1997; Ponton & Confessore, 1998). One of these behaviors is an active-approach to problem solving whereby the self-directed learner assumes the responsibility of developing solution strategies to problems that interfere with the learning activity. A weakness in the ability to perform this behavior could reduce the probability of a successful self-directed learning activity. Therefore, a diagnosis of this weakness may lead to a successful intervention that improves problem-solving abilities thus leading to mastery experiences that increase self-efficacy to perform self-directed learning. With these experiences, self-directed learning becomes a viable option in attaining desired outcomes.

Concluding Remarks

One should note that the proposed model is a quasi-linear perspective of a nonlinear behavioral process. Cognition resulting in self-influence occurs throughout the model, not just in the belief category. Behaviors, personal characteristics, and the environment interact reciprocally where changes in each determinant occur from one moment to the next. Behaviors provide input to general and contextual beliefs. Social learning via vicarious modeling also provides input into one's belief structure. The model is by no means all-inclusive but rather a method of framing behaviors with a particular focus on self-directed learning.

A salient goal of structured education is to increase the ability of departing students to successfully engage in self-directed learning activities. Within the framework of this model, self-directed learning must be understood by the individual to be a viable option in attaining desired outcomes from life. For this to occur, the person must not only be self-efficacious but also must have the requisite skills to engage in mastery experiences.

It becomes imperative that the educator works to develop within each learner the concept that ability is of dynamical proportions and can be increased with diligent efforts. Therefore, even less than successful learning activities are interpreted as processes in which learning ability increases along with enhanced self-efficacy. This perceived as well as actual increase in skills improves the expectation within the individual that self-directed learning is a viable means to desired ends. Such a realization can ultimately increase the productivity of any organization as well as the personal satisfaction derived from a fulfilling life.

References

Baker, G. L., & Gollub, J. P. (1990). *Chaotic dynamics: An introduction*. Cambridge, MA: Cambridge University Press.

Bandura, A. (1965). Behavioral modifications through modeling procedures. In L. Krasner & L. P. Ullmann (Eds.), *Research in behavior modification* (pp. 310-340). New York, NY: Holt, Rinehart and Winston.

Bandura, A. (1977a). Self-efficacy: Toward a unifying theory of behavioral change. *Psychological Review, 84*(2), 191-215.

Bandura, A. (1977b). *Social learning theory*. Englewood Cliffs, NJ: Prentice-Hall.

Bandura, A. (1997). *Self-efficacy: The exercise of control*. New York, NY: W. H. Freeman and Company.

Chapman, M., & Skinner, E. A. (1985). Action in development—Development in action. In M. Frese & J. Sabini (Eds.), *Goal-directed behavior: The concept of action in psychology* (pp. 200-213). Hillsdale, NJ: Lawrence Erlbaum Associates.

Confessore, G. J. (1992). An introduction to the study of self-directed learning. In G. J. Confessore & S. J. Confessore (Eds.), *Guideposts to self-directed learning: Expert commentary on essential concepts* (pp. 1-6). King of Prussia, PA: Organization Design and Development.

Covey, S. R. (1989). *The 7 habits of highly effective people: Powerful lessons in personal change*. New York, NY: Simon & Schuster.

Fishbein, M., & Ajzen, I. (1975). *Belief, attitude, intention, and behavior: An introduction to theory and research*. Reading, MA: Addison-Wesley.

Frese, M. (1997). Dynamic self-reliance: An important concept for work in the twenty-first century. In C. L. Cooper & S. E. Jackson (Eds.), *Creating tomorrow's organizations: A handbook for future research in organizational behavior* (pp. 399-416). New York, NY: John Wiley & Sons.

Frese, M., Kring, W., Soose, A., & Zempel, J. (1996). Personal initiative at work: Differences between East and West Germany. *Academy of Management Journal, 39*(2), 37-63.

Frese, M., & Sabini, J. (1985). Action theory: An introduction. In M. Frese & J. Sabini (Eds.), *Goal-directed behavior: The concept of action in psychology* (pp. xvii-xxv). Hillsdale, NJ: Lawrence Erlbaum Associates.

Frohman, A. L. (1997). Igniting organizational change from below: The power of personal initiative. *Organizational Dynamics, 25*(3), 39-53.

Gove, P. B. (Ed.). (1976). *Webster's third new international dictionary of the English language: Unabridged.* Springfield, MA: G. & C. Webster.

Hiemstra, R. (1994). Self-directed learning. In T. Husen & T. N. Postlethwaite (Eds.), *The international encyclopedia of education* (2nd ed.). Oxford, UK: Pergamon Press.

Howard, K. W. (1989). A comprehensive expectancy motivation model: Implications for adult education and training. *Adult Education Quarterly, 39*(4), 199-210.

Long, H. B. (1998). Theoretical and practical implications of selected paradigms of self-directed learning. In H. B. Long & Associates (Eds.), *Developing paradigms for self-directed learning* (pp. 1-14). Norman, OK: Public Managers Center, College of Education, University of Oklahoma.

Oddi, L. F. (1987). Perspectives on self-directed learning. *Adult Education Quarterly, 38*(1), 21-31.

Ponton, M. K., & Confessore, G. J. (1998). *Characteristics behaviors of personal initiative: A conate associated with self-directed learning.* Paper presented at the 12th International Symposium on Self-Directed Learning, Kissimmee, FL.

Popplestone, J. A., & McPherson, M. W. (1988). *Dictionary of concepts in general psychology.* Westport, CT: Greenwood Press.

Rosenbaum, M. (1989). Self-control under stress: The role of learned resourcefulness. *Advances in Behaviour Research and Therapy, 11*, 249-258.

Schroeder, M. (1991). *Fractals, chaos, power laws: Minutes from an infinite paradise*. New York, NY: W. H. Freeman and Company.

Tough, A. (1982). The other 80 percent of learning. In R. Gross (Ed.), *Invitation to lifelong learning* (pp. 153-157). Chicago, IL: Follett.

Vaill, P. B. (1996). *Learning as a way of being: Strategies for survival in a world of permanent white water*. San Francisco, CA: Jossey-Bass.

Volk, T. (1995). *Metapatterns: Across space, time, and mind*. New York, NY: Columbia University Press.

CHAPTER 2

UNDERSTANDING AND PROMOTING AUTONOMY IN SELF-DIRECTED LEARNING[2]

Three conations, initiative, resourcefulness, and persistence, have been proposed as being salient characteristic manifestations of autonomous learning. This chapter will attempt to define these constructs while proposing methods that educators may take in facilitating their enactment. This theoretical treatment is based upon published literature associated with the fields of self-directed learning and psychology and concludes with the proposition that while fostering learner autonomy is not often pedagogically considered, it is both possible and desirable for an educator to foster autonomy within students through the structured inculcation of the cognitive processes related to these conative factors.

The importance of self-directed learning as a discipline rests in its far-reaching effects on our society of learners. Tough (1982) estimated that approximately 80% of adult learners initiate self-directed learning activities. Without question, the respective contexts of these learning activities cover a spectrum from work related to recreational needs. Professors often feel that if their students (many of whom are barely in the classification of adulthood) were more "self-directed" in their learning, then not only would they be better prepared for the courses that are offered but they would also maximize the eventual benefits of their formal education.

However the term "self-directed learning" is used to describe many types of learning activities thereby existing without a unique definition (Ponton, Carr, & Confessore, 2000). According to Oddi (1987) and Merriam and Caffarella (1999), self-directed learning research can be dichotomized into two broad categories: a process perspective or a personality characteristic perspective. Furthermore, these authors

---

[2]This article is reprinted from *Current Research in Social Psychology* [2000, 5(19)]

asserted that the process perspective is the dominant viewpoint that has been adopted by researchers within the field.

The process perspective generally focuses on the activities that the learner engages in such as goal setting, planning a learning strategy, acquiring resources, and monitoring progress (Knowles, 1975; Oddi, 1987). These activities parallel what Zimmerman, Bonner, and Kovach (1996) referred to as "self-regulation" where self-regulation refers to the self-generated activities, both cognitive and behavioral, that a person uses to accomplish their educational goals. However, these activities are predicated on the psychological situation of the learner. As Knowles (1980) stated,

> Learning is described psychologically as a process of need-meeting and goal-striving by the learners. This is to say that individuals are motivated to engage in learning to the extent that they feel a need to learn and perceive a personal goal that learning will help to achieve; and they will invest their energy in making use of available resources (including teachers and readings) to the extent that they perceive them as being relevant to their needs and goals. (p. 56)

These ideas are congruent with Long (1989) who asserted that self-directed learning can be conceptualized along a sociological dimension (addressing learner isolation), a pedagogical dimension (addressing the learner's activities), or a psychological dimension (addressing the learner's mental state). The process description of self-directed learning encompasses both the sociological and pedagogical dimensions. However, Long (1998) asserted that only "the *psychological conceptualization* is both necessary and sufficient to explain SDL [self-directed learning]" (p. 10). He stated the following:

> The psychological conceptualization implies that fundamentally learning is a self-initiated, self-directed, and self-regulated cognitive process whereby the learner can choose to ignore instruction, to merely absorb it by casual attention, to carefully memorize without critical reflection, or to seek to change or create an understanding of information. (p. 9)

One aspect of the psychological dimension consists of the learner identifying needs that serve as motivational inducements to cogitate learning goals. Another aspect of this dimension is the learner's personality characteristics.

Imagine two students working diligently in their university library on a Friday night. They appear to be involved in similar activities: finding material, reading books and articles, taking notes, evaluating their information and seeking additional information. However, there is an important difference between them. The first student is there because he has procrastinated for several weeks and now has an assignment that is due on Monday. The second student is there because she happens to be curious about a topic that a professor casually mentioned during the course of a lecture. This difference can be found in the concept of *learner autonomy*.

The concept of autonomy (Knowles, 1980; Merriam & Caffarella, 1999) exists under the personality characteristic perspective of self-directed learning. Chene (1983) defined learner autonomy in terms of independence. Such independence is based upon an individual's personal will to learn something of perceived value that results in the learner's discretion of how to best accomplish the desired level of learning. Thus, learner autonomy can be defined as the characteristic of the person who independently exhibits agency (i.e., intentional actions) in learning activities (Ponton 1999) where independence is the characteristic of the person who controls his or her own actions, control being "a state of mind, as well as of one's environment" (Sheldon & Elliot, 1998, p. 546).

Now while both of the students mentioned above exhibit some degree of autonomy (after all, *it is* a Friday night), the major differences between them are not solely in the process of self-directed learning (i.e., identifying a learning goal, planning a learning strategy, gathering learning resources, and evaluating learning progress) but rather in that these processes represents manifestations related to their personality characteristics as a learner (i.e., the second student has independently chosen to learn something of perceived value). These manifestations represent *autonomous learning* (i.e., *learner autonomy* can be viewed as the psychological undergirding that leads to the behaviors associated with the process of *autonomous learning*) that include initiative, resourcefulness, and persistence (Confessore, 1991) referred to as conative factors because the manifestation of each is predicated on an individual's desire to engage in a learning activity. (Note that *conative* is used to describe the determination to engage in an activity or reach a future desired state, i.e., intentional.) Confessore (1991) further asserted that individuals who exhibit these conative factors in their learning activities "possess traits which are essential to successful self-direction in learning" (p. 129). Using the dichotomy of process and personality characteristic perspectives of autonomous learning can be misleading because the learning processes attributed to the behaviors of autonomous learning are manifest as a result of the learner's personality characteristics of autonomy.

For an educator to promote autonomy within his or her students requires an understanding of initiative, resourcefulness, and persistence and methods of development. It is suggested that promoting autonomous learning (i.e., the exhibition of initiative, resourcefulness, and persistence) will develop learner autonomy because of the valued outcomes that will follow; that is, autonomy will not only enhance students' formal educational experience but will also provide them with the psychological undergirding essential for lifelong learning. The purpose of this chapter is twofold: to clarify the conative factors associated with autonomous learning and to suggest ways in which an educator can promote the development of autonomy within students.

Discussion

When one asserts that a student is "showing initiative" in his or her learning, what specific manifestations are being referred to? Based upon an understanding of personal initiative developed from research conducted in nonacademic environments (cf. Ghiselli, 1971; Hoehne, 1990; Frese, Kring, Soose, & Zempel, 1996; Frohman, 1997), Ponton (1999) defined the theoretical construct of personal initiative in autonomous learning as a behavioral syndrome (i.e., a group of co-occurring behaviors) consisting of the following five behaviors: goal-directedness, action-orientation, active-approach to problem solving, persistence in overcoming obstacles, and self-startedness.

Goal-directedness refers to establishing learning goals and working toward their accomplishment. Specific and challenging goals are important to induce motivation because of the anticipated self-satisfaction that will occur when goals are realized (Bandura, 1997). In addition, while adopting long range goals provides a general direction to work toward, the establishment and accomplishment of proximal subgoals provide the learner with immediate feedback thereby facilitating an assessment as to whether the adopted learning strategies are enabling the learner to reach the ultimate distal goal.

However learning goals are adopted because of the perceived value of anticipated outcomes that will follow when goals are accomplished. Such valued outcomes may be personal (e.g., pleasure), social (e.g., respect from valued others, money), or self-evaluative (e.g., the satisfaction from behaviors meeting self-standards of performance; Bandura, 1997). Therefore, to facilitate goal-directedness, educators need to help students understand the positive correlation between specific learning goals and the outcomes that the students desire from their formal education. Humans are cognitively motivated to engage in activities directed at accomplishing specific goals when they value the expected outcomes that will likely follow, which is the basic premise of expectancy value theory (Atkinson, 1982; Vroom, 1964). Afterwards, students should be encouraged to establish their own specific and challenging goals while educators continually facilitate within them with the learning skills necessary to accomplish these goals thereby enabling them to further the development of their individual learning skills.

When a student intends on learning something, the rapidity with which this intention is transformed into a learning activity is referred to as *action-orientation*. Chapman and Skinner (1985) stated, "the intentionality of action implies a differentiation of ends and means . . . [whereby] the action is performed *in order* to bring about a certain goal" (p. 201). Thus, a person displaying initiative will be both goal-directed and action-oriented (Frese et al., 1996).

Frese and Sabini (1985) asserted that "according to action theory, there must be at least a general notion of a goal and a general plan before on is able to act at all" (p. xx). This implies that when a student identifies some desired level of learning (i.e., a learning goal), the student must formulate a general plan on how to best accomplish the learning. A goal of formal education is to develop learning skills within students thereby providing them with a repertoire of learning tools to choose from depending upon the context of the desired learning. However, it is incumbent upon the educator to guide the student as to which tools are appropriate for which learning. As an example, reading current conference articles or conversing with working professionals as opposed to reading journals or books best facilitates topical learning. Even the techniques required in finding desired information may be an important skill for the student to acquire. If so, educators should provide learning exercises that require students to find relevant information, compare and contrast content, while continually providing corrective modeling instructing how to best extract important ideas.

Ultimately, skill development and the organization of such skills (a.k.a. planning) in accomplishing desired levels of learning will equip the student with the means to plan learning activities expeditiously and efficiently thereby facilitating an action-orientation.

Self-startedness, the behavior of motivating oneself to begin a learning activity, occurs when the student is able to identify desired outcomes, create goals, develop plans, and work toward goal accomplishment independently. "Such [self] motivation emerges spontaneously from internal tendencies and can motivate behavior even without the aid of extrinsic rewards or environmental controls" (Deci & Ryan, 1985, p. 43). A self-starting behavior, while facilitated by valued expected outcomes and the anticipated self-satisfaction of accomplishing challenging goals, is also influenced by the perceived presence of obstacles.

Blankenship (1985) stated the following:

> The initial activities associated with the dominance of an intentional action tendency would be characterized as the OTIUM [opportunity, time, importance, urgency, means] checks that would either result in the repeated inhibition and immediate decrease of the ongoing action tendency, if OTIUM criteria were not met, or result in the additional instigation of the action tendency and withdrawal of previous inhibitory force, if the OTIUM criteria were met. (p. 168)

The importance check refers to "reflecting on the positive aspects of goal attainment" (Heckhausen & Kuhl, 1985, p. 153) and is facilitated when educators help students to understand the positive correlation between the accomplishment of learning goals and the realization of desired outcomes (see *goal-directedness* above). In addition, the means check is related to learning skill development as well as the ability to plan learning activities that accomplish desired levels of learning as previously discussed.

The ability of learners to perceive that opportunity, time, and urgency are present is predicated upon their *active-approach to problem solving*. An active-approach refers to the behavior of taking the responsibility for the development of solution strategies to one's own problems. The deterrents to learning may come in many forms (cf. Darkenwald & Valentine, 1985) some of which are a lack of resources (i.e., lack of opportunity), time constraints (i.e., lack of time), and a low priority of learning as compared to other activities (i.e., lack of urgency). An important goal for the educator is to convey to students that it is their responsibility to show an active-approach in their learning by taking the responsibility to create learning opportunities (e.g., seeking learning resources, designating learning environments), reserving time dedicated solely to learning activities, and create urgency in their learning (i.e., prioritizing learning above other activities) through the realization that the learning opportunities afforded by formal education are often limited in duration.

When students realize that it is their responsibility to both solve the problems that impede desired levels of learning and to become suitably armed with a repertoire of learning and planning skills, then *persistence in overcoming obstacles* becomes an anticipated behavior. Yet such persistence is highly influenced by a student's perception of his or her perseverant capability, referred to as self-efficacy (Bandura, 1997). As a student continually performs OTIUM checks and learning activities, instead of nonlearning activities, are pursued through the creation of opportunity, time, importance, urgency or means, then the student learns via these mastery experiences (Bandura, 1977) that he or she has the skill to successfully overcome learning obstacles. This process is facilitated when educators recognize the presence of these obstacles and encourage students to take the responsibility to use acquired skills (such as planning) or develop new skills (such as time management) to satisfy OTIUM criteria. Because everyone performs the OTIUM checks in choosing which activities to pursue, educators should encourage students to observe the behaviors of successful models and pattern their actions in creating opportunity, time, importance, urgency and means in their learning activities. When such models are chosen from similar others such as student peers, then self-efficacy may be enhanced vicariously; that is, when people that we perceive to be like us show capability, we often believe that we are equally capable of performing at similar levels.

As a behavior of initiative, persistence refers to the continuation of action in spite of the presence of obstacles. As Frohman (1997) asserted, "if there is one element that describes those who successfully take personal initiative, it is their dogged sense of purpose, commitment to keep going, and understanding that it takes time" (p. 47). However, perseverant behavior is also congruent with the concept of volition (Derrick, 2001) where volition is a postdecisional process whereby once one decides (i.e., intends) to engage in a behavior, volition refers to the maintenance of motivation in proceeding from intention to behavior. As Heckhausen and Kuhl (1985) stated:

> Motivation refers to all elaborations of values and expectancies and their integration. Once the elaborating processes of motivation have run their course or have ceased, leaving behind an invitation to action, self-commitment initiates the volition process that leads to an eventual enactment of the resulting intention in due time and at the appropriate occasion. (p. 151)

Kuhl and Fuhrmann (1998) indicated that volition has two aspects, self-control and self-regulation, and that one's level of commitment to maintain participation in a behavior is related to the degree to which both of these forms of volition are present. They asserted, "the mode of volition supporting the maintenance of an active goal is called *self-control* . . . whereas the mode supporting the task of maintaining one's actions in line with one's integrated self [i.e., the person's self-concept of who he or she is] is called *self-regulation*" (p. 15).

Carr's (1999) concept of resourcefulness in autonomous learning is based upon the volitional process of self-control as previously defined by Rosenbaum (1989). Learner resourcefulness consists of the activation of four behaviors: anticipating the future rewards of learning, prioritizing learning over other activities, delaying immediate gratification, and solving problems in one's learning (Carr, 1999). The degree to which a learner is deemed resourceful in autonomous learning is related to the degree to which these four behaviors are manifest thereby enabling the learner to actively pursue his or her learning goal. The term "resourceful" is used because conceptually resourcefulness is used to describe a person who is capable of dealing with problematic situations that induce stress. Learning activities can induce stress not only from the perspective of the learner having to extend capability or understanding but also from the decisions that have to be made concerning which activities to pursue caused by competing activities that vie for the learner's time and energy. In general, stress refers to "any *internal* event such as anxiety, pain, or thought that disrupts the effective performance of a target behavior" (Rosenbaum, 1980, p. 110).

The four resourceful behaviors are highly interrelated (which may be expected for a unified construct) and are interrelated with personal initiative as well (which also may be expected due to their supportive roles in autonomous learning). As already mentioned, to facilitate goal-directedness the educator should highlight to the student the positive correlation between the accomplishment of learning/course goals and the valued outcomes that will likely follow. By internalizing this correlation, the student will be better able to engage in the resourceful behavior of *anticipating future rewards*. The student will then *prioritize learning over other activities* due to this anticipated benefit even if it involves *delaying the immediate gratification* that may be realized from participating in nonlearning activities. Also, the development of learning and planning skills has been highlighted as being critical if a student is expected to be action-oriented in his or her learning activities. Such skill development is of paramount importance in being able to *solve the problems* associated with the development and completion of a learning activity.

In addition to planning, problem solving encompasses evaluating alternatives and anticipating consequences (Ponton, Carr, & Confessore, 2000). This evaluation and anticipation is best promoted when the educator models problem solving behaviors in classroom exercises and later internalized when students are tasked to conduct learning on their own thereby gaining experience that not only improves their ability to solve learning problems but also improves their self-perception that they are capable of learning what they desire when they desire (i.e., increases self-efficacy in autonomous learning). This latter realization is crucial to the development of lifelong learners. The importance of resourcefulness with respect to persistence is that by exhibiting self-control in learning, students are able to focus on the value of learning activities (thereby choosing learning activities over nonlearning activities that may, in the short term, be more pleasurable) and solve the problems that interfere with their desired levels of learning thereby enhancing perseverant tendencies.

The second volitional process important to persistent behavior is self-regulation. Zimmerman, Bonner, and Kovach (1996) provided a cyclic model of self-regulated learning that involves the following processes: self-evaluation and monitoring, goal setting and strategic planning, strategy implementation and monitoring, and strategic outcome monitoring (p. 11). *Self-evaluation and monitoring* occur when the student compares current levels of learning to desired levels. Educators facilitate this process when the value of anticipated course outcomes is conveyed to students and an accurate assessment is performed to indicate the discrepancy between the students' current and desired levels of achievement. Typically, this process of evaluation occurs whenever periodic assessments are performed. However, the ultimate goal of this process is for students to develop the requisite skills to independently identify desired learning outcomes and be able to not only identify discrepancies between current and desired future states but also anticipate the effectiveness of potential learning strategies based upon past performances. *Goal setting and strategic planning* refer to the activity of establishing learning goals and planning learning activities that will hopefully lead to desirable learning outcomes. As already mentioned, autonomous goal setting and planning skills are developed through the evaluation of the effectiveness of past learning strategies of goal setting and planning; strategies that were initially modeled by the educator but later tasked to the student in course-related activities. After a plan is developed, *strategic implementation and monitoring* refer to the implementation of the plan and an evaluation as to the accuracy of the implementation. As a simple example, students who establish a plan of reading the notes from a particular course for one hour every night need to monitor their efforts (e.g., create a reading log) to determine if, in fact, they are actually reading for the intended duration. Establishing a specific plan and methods of evaluating implementation represent a specific goal in itself thereby providing motivation due to the clear discrepancy between current and desired states. *Strategic outcome monitoring* refers to the process in which the learner makes determinations as to whether adopted goals and plans are leading to desired outcomes. In class, the educator facilitates this process by helping students to understand the desirable learning outcomes at the beginning of the semester, the connection between course goals and the outcomes, why the course format best facilitates the accomplishment of the goals, and then at the end of the semester that the desirable outcomes have been realized thereby feeding directly into the beginning process of the cycle, namely self-evaluation and monitoring. In autonomous learning activities, these two processes (i.e., *strategic outcome* and *self-evaluation and monitoring*) are critical in providing feedback as to whether or not adopted goals and plans are adequate for the eventual levels of desired learning. Students need to be encouraged to reflect upon outcomes, goals, and strategies thereby reinforcing the importance of the self-regulation process.

Self-regulation is a critical cyclic process of persistence in autonomous learning because it represents the necessary activities required in any successful learning activity. The autonomy rests in the learner's ability to initiate these processes independently subsequent to successful modeling activities provided by the educator.

Concluding Remarks

The development of lifelong learners as a goal of formalized education is not a new idea (although some might think so due to the popularity of the term). Professors recognize that the content material that they offer to their students is merely foundational in that the actual needs of ultimate vocations will be met with new knowledge that is built upon the foundation created in college. The hope is that enough of a curriculum is provided to create a good starting point for future learning from the perspectives of salient content mastery and acquired skill in learning.

Yet fostering autonomy in students is not often pedagogically considered. It is not enough for students to "know" certain things (i.e., content mastery) and be able to "do" certain things (i.e., skill mastery); they must also want to know more things and be able to muster the requisite cognitive inducements to exhibit personal initiative, resourcefulness, and persistence in their learning. As Dewey (1916) asserted:

> If he [i.e., the student] cannot devise his own solution
> (not of course in isolation, but in correspondence with
> the teacher and other pupils) and find his own way out
> he will not learn, not even if he can recite some correct
> answer with one hundred per cent accuracy. We can
> and do supply ready-made "ideas" by the thousand; we
> do not usually take much pains to see that the one
> learning engages in significant situations where his
> own activities generate, support, and clinch ideas—
> that is, perceived meanings or connections. (p. 160)

Educators must work to inculcate the necessary cognitive processes that promote students to develop their "own solution" to problems. This chapter has presented many of these cognitive processes: valuing learning as a means to desired outcomes, understanding that the accomplishment of suitably chosen goals can lead to desired outcomes, and assuming responsibility for one's own learning. Based upon these prerequisite processes, additional processes are enlisted such as prioritizing learning over other activities; self-evaluating current states to future desired states of learning; creating suitable learning goals and plans; monitoring whether planned learning activities are leading to desired outcomes; adjusting plans accordingly; solving the problems that interfere with learning; and creating the opportunity, time, importance, urgency, and means for one's own learning activities. These processes can be reinforced within the student regardless of educational level or the instructional environment (including distance education).

When students can autonomously initiate these processes without mandates or even encouragement from others primarily due to attributions of feelings of control over past learning successes, then educators have been truly successful in "educating" their students. As Dewey (1916) stated, "the inclination to learn from life itself and to make the conditions of life such that all will learn in the process of living is the finest product of schooling" (p. 51). The skills of educators are not complete until they understand, and are able to promote, autonomy in self-directed learning thereby enhancing their students' capability to engage in lifelong learning as individual desires evolve. The influence of education on students need not and should not stop when the formal curriculum is completed.

References

Atkinson, J. W. (1982). Old and new conceptions of how expected consequences influence actions. In N. T. Feather (Ed.), *Expectations and actions: Expectancy-value models in psychology* (pp. 17-52). Hillsdale, NJ: Lawrence Erlbaum Associates.

Bandura, A. (1997). *Self-efficacy: The exercise of control.* New York, NY: W. H. Freeman and Company.

Blankenship, V. (1985). The dynamics of intention. In M. Frese & J. Sabini (Eds.), *Goal- directed behavior: The concept of action in psychology* (pp. 161-170). Hillsdale, NJ: Lawrence Erlbaum Associates.

Carr, P. B. (1999). *The measurement of resourcefulness intentions in the adult autonomous learner* (Unpublished doctoral dissertation). The George Washington University, Washington, DC.

Chapman, M., & Skinner, E. A. (1985). Action in development—Development in action. In M. Frese & J. Sabini (Eds.), *Goal-directed behavior: The concept of action in psychology* (pp. 200-213). Hillsdale, NJ: Lawrence Erlbaum Associates.

Chene, A. (1983). The concept of autonomy in adult education: A philosophical discussion. *Adult Education Quarterly, 34*, 38-47.

Confessore, G. J. (1991). Human behavior as a construct for assessing Guglielmino's self-directed learning readiness scale: Pragmatism revisited. In H. B. Long & Associates (Eds.), *Self-directed learning: Consensus and conflict* (pp. 123-146). Norman, OK: Oklahoma Research Center for Continuing Professional and Higher Education of the University of Oklahoma.

Darkenwald, G. G., & Valentine, T. (1985). Factor structure of deterrents to public participation in adult education. *Adult Education Quarterly, 35*, 177-193.

Deci, E. L., & Ryan, R. M. (1985). *Intrinsic motivation and self-determination in human behavior.* New York, NY: Plenum Press.

Derrick, M. G. (2001). *The measurement of an adult's intention to exhibit persistence in autonomous learning* (Unpublished doctoral dissertation). The George Washington University, Washington, DC.

Dewey, J. (1916). *Democracy and education.* New York, NY: Macmillan.

Frese, M., Kring, W., Soose, A., & Zempel, J. (1996). Personal initiative at work: Differences between East and West Germany. *Academy of Management Journal, 39*, 37-63.

Frese, M., & Sabini, J. (1985). Action theory: An introduction. In M. Frese & J. Sabini (Eds.), *Goal directed behavior: The concept of action in psychology* (pp. xvii-xxv). Hillsdale, NJ: Lawrence Erlbaum Associates.

Frohman, A. L. (1997). Igniting organizational change from below: The power of personal initiative. *Organizational Dynamics, 25*, 39-53.

Ghiselli, E. E. (1971). *Explorations in managerial talent.* Pacific Palisades, CA: Goodyear.

Heckhausen, H., & Kuhl, J. (1985). From wishes to action: The dead ends and short cuts on the long way to action. In M. Frese & J. Sabini (Eds.), *Goal-directed behavior: The concept of action in psychology* (pp. 134-157). Hillsdale, NJ: Lawrence Erlbaum Associates.

Hoehne, K. A. K. (1990). Initiative-a neglected psychosocial dimension. *Social Psychiatry and Psychiatric Epidemiology, 25*, 101-107.

Knowles, M. S. (1975). *Self-directed learning: A guide for learners and teachers.* Chicago, IL: Follett.

Knowles, M. S. (1980). *The modern practice of adult education: From pedagogy to andragogy.* New York, NY: Cambridge Books.

Kuhl, J., & Fuhrmann, A. (1998). Decomposing self-regulation and self-control: The Volitional Components Inventory. In J. Heckhausen & C. Dweck (Eds.), *Lifespan perspectives on motivation and control* (pp. 15-49). Hillsdale, NJ: Lawrence Erlbaum Associates.

Long, H. B. (1989). Self-directed learning: Emerging theory and practice. In H. B. Long & Associates (Eds.), *Self-directed learning: Emerging theory and practice* (pp. 1-11). Norman, OK: Oklahoma Research Center for Continuing Professional and Higher Education of the University of Oklahoma.

Long, H. B. (1998). Theoretical and practical implications of selected paradigms of self-directed learning. In H. B. Long & Associates (Eds.), *Developing paradigms for self-directed learning* (pp. 1-14). Norman, OK: Public Managers Center, College of Education, University of Oklahoma.

Merriam, S. B., & Caffarella, R. S. (1999). *Learning in adulthood: A comprehensive guide* (2nd ed.). San Francisco, CA: Jossey-Bass.

Oddi, L. F. (1987). Perspectives on self-directed learning. *Adult Education Quarterly, 38,* 21-31.

Ponton, M. K. (1999). *The measurement of an adult's intention to exhibit personal initiative in autonomous learning* (Unpublished doctoral dissertation). The George Washington University, Washington, DC.

Ponton, M. K., Carr, P. B., & Confessore, G. J. (2000). Learning conation: A psychological perspective of personal initiative and resourcefulness. In H. B. Long & Associates (Eds.), *Practice and theory in self-directed learning* (pp. 65-82). Schaumburg, IL: Motorola University Press.

Rosenbaum, M. (1980). A schedule for assessing self-control behaviors: Preliminary findings. *Behavior Therapy, 11,* 109-121.

Rosenbaum, M. (1989). Self-control under stress: The role of learned resourcefulness. *Advances in Behaviour Research and Therapy, 11,* 249-258.

Sheldon, K. M., & Elliot, A. J. (1998). Not all personal goals are personal: Comparing autonomous and controlled reasons for goals as predictors of effort and attainment. *Personality and Social Psychology Bulletin, 24,* 546-557.

Tough, A. (1982). The other 80 percent of learning. In R. Gross (Ed.), *Invitation to lifelong learning* (pp. 153-157). Chicago, IL: Follett.

Vroom, V. H. (1964). *Work and motivation.* New York, NY: John Wiley and Sons.

Zimmerman, B. J., Bonner, S., & Kovach, R. (1996). *Developing self-regulated learners: Beyond achievement to self-efficacy.* Washington, DC: American Psychological Association.

CHAPTER 3

AUTONOMOUS LEARNING FROM A SOCIAL COGNITIVE PERSPECTIVE[3]

The current perspective of autonomous learning defines it as the agentic exhibition of resourcefulness, initiative, and persistence in self-directed learning. As a form of human agency, it has been argued in the literature that this perspective should be consistent with Bandura's (1986) Social Cognitive Theory (SCT). The purpose of this chapter is to present an alignment between salient aspects of autonomous learning theory and SCT thereby providing a heuristic position that guides future research in adult learning. Topics such as self-efficacy, cognitive motivation, and conation will be addressed. In addition, current research from the literature in autonomous learning will be discussed.

In 1991, Confessore alluded to the importance of desire, resourcefulness, initiative, and persistence in self-directed learning. Since that time, researchers (Carr, 1999; Derrick, 2001; Meyer, 2001; Ponton, 1999; Ponton & Carr, 2000; Ponton, Carr, & Derrick, 2004) have attempted to theoretically define these constructs within the context of adult autonomous learning. Because autonomous learning was conceptualized as an agentic activity (Ponton, 1999), the study of associated conative factors led to a review of Bandura's (1986) Social Cognitive Theory (SCT). Unlike radical behaviorism or cognitivism, SCT recognizes that human behavior is intentional and is influenced by the environment and cognitive processes. Modeled as an intentional behavior, autonomous learning, as well as any description of its enactment, must be consistent with SCT.

Thus, a current conceptualization of autonomous learning states that it represents an agentic process resulting in the manifestation of resourcefulness (Carr, 1999), initiative (Ponton, 1999), and persistence (Derrick, 2001) in one's learning. Such agency is predicated upon the learner's (i.e., the agent's) beliefs and attitudes which generate

---

[3]This article is reprinted with permission from *New Horizons in Adult Education and Human Resource Development* and is copyrighted © John Wiley and Sons [2006, *20*(2), 38-49]

behavioral intentions and subsequent behaviors (cf. Fishbein & Ajzen, 1975). Therefore, cognition and affection play a paramount role in conation (Fishbein & Ajzen, 1975) unlike earlier theories of behaviorism that discount the role of thinking upon action (Bugelski, 1964). Consistent with SCT, autonomous learning results from interplay among the environment, the person, and behaviors and is the mechanism through which self-motivated personal development is realized.

Further research is required to develop adequate models of autonomous learning that serve to guide those interested in developing facilitative strategies. Developing such models will require the measurement of variables related to human agency within the context of adult learning. Thus, the purpose of this chapter is to present an alignment between salient aspects of autonomous learning theory and SCT thereby providing a heuristic position that guides future research in adult learning. The theoretical alignment suggested will be based upon a synthesis of extant literature rather than original research. The question that guides this discussion is the following: What SCT concepts inform autonomous learning theory?

This chapter will first present SCT related concepts such as the constituent forms of human functioning, triadic reciprocal causation, agency, self-efficacy, and cognitive motivation (Bandura, 1986, 1997). Next the simple behavioral model of Fishbein and Ajzen (1975) relating beliefs, attitudes, intentions, and behaviors will be presented followed by Ponton and Carr's (1999) expansion of this model to self-directed learning. The current conceptualization of autonomous learning theory will be explained next and then interpreted using a SCT lens. Recent research (Ponton, Carr, et al., 2004; Ponton, Derrick, & Carr, 2005; Ponton, Derrick, Carr, & Hall, 2004) that informs practice will be presented next followed by summary remarks.

Social Cognitive Theory: Basic Concepts

A basic premise of Bandura's (1986) Social Cognitive Theory is that humans are motivated to engage in different activities due to cognitive processes that use information resulting from either personal action or the observed actions of others. To support these performance related mechanisms, SCT recognizes five forms of human functioning: symbolization, forethought, vicarious learning, self-regulation, and self-reflection (Bandura, 1986). Symbolization refers to a person's ability to create mental images of temporary sensory experiences or information stored in long term memory. Forethought is the ability to use symbolization to create mentally unrealized future scenarios that provide motivation and desirable courses to pursue. Vicarious learning represents the ability to learn from others—a mechanism that allows our society to continually advance the knowledge base by not wasting time relearning the same lessons but also eliminating serious safety risks in having to relearn lessons with life threatening consequences. Self-regulation enables a person to select and manage pertinent activities in order to realize goals. Lastly, self-reflection refers to a person's ability to think about the consequences of past experiences thereby shaping subsequent beliefs, attitudes, intentions, and behaviors. As evident from these inherent human capabilities, SCT recognizes the primacy of thought in action.

Furthermore, SCT acknowledges that factors associated with environment, person, and behavior exert influence over the aforementioned forms of human functioning (Bandura, 1986). The environment represents the physical world; the person represents internal cognitive, affective, conative, and biological processes; and behaviors are the actions of the agent. Through what Bandura (1986) termed triadic reciprocal causation, these three factors bidirectionally influence human functioning relative to the situation presented and the person involved. As an example, identical environmental factors with respect to a specific activity may be interpreted by one person as insurmountable thus leading to activity avoidance but interpreted by another as a requirement to invoke coping strategies when performing this activity. The variation in agency is due to interpretive differences between the two individuals.

Three distinct forms of agency can be modeled: mechanical, autonomous, and emergent interactive (Bandura, 1989). Mechanical agency describes the situation in which the environment determines action independent of cognitive influence, a premise consistent with radical behaviorism. Autonomous agency describes situations in which thought, independent of the environment, determines actions, a concept associated with radical cognitivism. SCT rejects the first two forms of agency and supports a third form, emergent interactive agency, that emphasizes the concept that human functioning is determined by all three factors—person, environment, and behavior—working interdependently (i.e., triadic reciprocal causation; Bandura, 1986). SCT, then, is built upon the premise that human performance is a consequence of interactive factors. Thought, environment, and behavior exert varying degrees of influence on individual performance relative to specific tasks.

Social Cognitive Theory: Related Concepts

Self-Efficacy

The notion that cognition influences behavior explains the influential role of self-efficacy, which is the personal perception of one's ability to successfully execute an activity (Bandura, 1997). As a perception, self-efficacy may or may not correspond to objective measures of capability; however, it plays a crucial mediating role in cognitive motivation and, thus, influences activity choice as well as perseverance required for goal completion. Personal assessments of efficacy include both context (i.e., specific activity in which capability is being considered) and strength (i.e., degree to which the perceived capability is believed to be present particularly when impediments are present).

As a perception (not in the sensory sense but in the cognitive evaluative sense), self-efficacy is an interpretation of oneself based upon the processing of information. In this regard, self-reflection is the form of functioning that influences efficacy assessments. Consistent with reciprocal determinism, the environment and behaviors provide the information that is interpreted by the person in assessing efficacy, where self-efficacy beliefs reside within the person. The reciprocal mechanism as modeled by triadic reciprocal causation is enacted when efficacy assessments affect the environment (via subjective interpretations of opportunities associated with activity choices and potential impediments to success) and behavior (via activity choice, performance, perseverance, and interpretation of resultant outcomes).

Behavior and environment provide four sources of efficacy information: mastery experiences, physiological/emotive arousals, vicarious experiences, and verbal persuasion (Bandura, 1997). The first two refer to interpretations of consequences related to personal behavior, whereas the last two refer to information supplied by the environment. Mastery experiences are past experiences with the same or similar activities that provide indicants of capability; physiological/emotive arousals are somatic/affective reactions to performances; vicarious experiences are the performances of similar others that provide information as to whether personal capability exists; verbal persuasion is an assessment from another concerning one's capability. The direction of influence of these four sources on efficacy (i.e., whether self-efficacy beliefs are strengthened or weakened), however, depends upon the individual's interpretation of the information provided. For instance, past successes attributed to outside facilitation (e.g., the help of others) rather than personal capability would not strengthen percepts of self-efficacy (Bandura, 1997).

Cognitive Motivation

The basic premise of expectancy value theory states that humans will be motivated to engage in behaviors that they perceive will lead to desirable outcomes or avoid aversive outcomes (Atkinson, 1964; Vroom, 1964). SCT (Bandura, 1997) characterizes these outcomes as personal (e.g., pleasure, pain), social (e.g., money, awards, ostracism, respect), or self-evaluative (i.e., consistency with self-standards of behavior). Desirable outcomes provide incentives to adopt performance goals and engage in behaviors that lead to these outcomes. Antithetically, undesirable outcomes render disincentives to engage in activities leading to them. Personal or self-evaluative incentives form the basis for intrinsic motivation whereas the basis for extrinsic motivation resides in social incentives (cf. Bandura, 1986). Self-efficacy mediates the influence of outcome expectancies on motivation as behaviors are not chosen unless the agent believes that requisite capability for success exists (Bandura, 1997); that is, people do not tend to engage in endeavors that they perceive as futile.

Performance goals, then, are targeted end states that an agent believes, if reached, will lead to one or several desirable outcomes (Bandura, 1997). Using forethought via symbolization, individuals consider various goals, evaluate courses of action, and formulate plans in order to achieve personally valued goals. The correlation between performance goals and desirable outcomes may be learned vicariously when personal experiences are absent. When an activity is chosen, an individual utilizes self-regulation to act toward the pre-established goal and utilizes self-reflection to evaluate actions in terms of goal achievement and desirable outcomes. Again, self-efficacy is influential in this process. Should individuals perceive themselves incapable of success, they will avoid the task regardless of possible desirable outcomes.

Self-reflective attributions that one makes concerning the causes for successes or failures influence the motivation to engage in similar activities in the future (Weiner, 1985). Mastery experiences will increase self-efficacy if successes are attributed to personal ability;

successes attributed to environmental factors will not (Bandura, 1997). Failures attributed to a lack of capability will reduce efficacy; failures attributed to a lack of effort will not (Bandura, 1997). In addition, self-efficacy influences causal attributions. Someone with strong efficacy beliefs is more likely to attribute successful performances to personal capability or failed performances to a lack of effort where such attributions will motivate the agent to choose similar activities in the future when past realized outcomes are again desirable.

Beliefs, Attitudes, Intentions, and Behaviors

According to Fishbein and Ajzen (1975), beliefs reciprocally influence attitudes where attitudes influence subsequent intention formulation and behavioral choices. Using a feedback model, the consequences of behaviors provide information for additional beliefs thereby perpetuating the cycle. Beliefs represent our knowledge of the world where different objects of thought (e.g., a person, place, event, behavior, or idea) are differentiated from other objects using distinguishing attributes. These attributive assignments may be subjective (i.e., not factual) and influenced by our attitudes toward the object of thought. Based upon these attributes and our attitudes toward these attributes as separate objects of thought, an individual may feel either favorable (i.e., a positive attitude) or unfavorable (i.e., a negative attitude) toward the object itself.

When the object of thought is a behavior, Fishbein and Ajzen (1975) asserted that a behavioral intention will develop if a favorable attitude toward the behavior exists. This will occur when (a) the behavior is believed to lead to desirable outcomes, (b) the behavior is encouraged by significant others, and (c) factors to facilitate the behavior exist (Ajzen, 2002). Blankenship (1985) asserted that intentions transform into behaviors when opportunity, time, importance, urgency, and means are perceived to exist whereas Frese and Sabini (1985) theorized that a wish precedes an intention, where a wish is a dormant intention that transforms into an intention when facilitative opportunities arise.

The model provided by Fishbein and Ajzen (1975) is consistent with SCT as it supports the decisional role of thought (cognition and affection) in activity choice (conation and behavior). Full congruency with triadic reciprocal causation would include an environmental factor as follows: (a) Information from the environment and from personal behavior influence beliefs and attitudes; (b) beliefs and attitudes result in subjective interpretations of the environment and in behaviors; and (c) the environment provides restrictions and/or opportunities for behaviors to occur whereas behaviors objectively transform the environment.

A Model of Self-Directed Learning

In 1999, Ponton and Carr presented a model of self-directed learning consistent with the aforementioned concepts (see Chapter 1, Figure 2). The Ponton and Carr model encompasses two dichotomous elements: (a) general and contextual applications, and (b) learner self-directedness and self-directed learning.

To understand the model, examination begins at the general beliefs location. General beliefs represent the entire universe of personal object-attribute assignments or everything an individual knows. These beliefs provide information upon which to develop attitudes toward various objects thus creating a personal value system. On the basis of this value system, individuals determine outcomes desired from life.

Once desired outcomes are identified, the individual proceeds to decisions regarding pertinent actions required for the outcomes to occur. At this point, decisions become more context-specific as specific behaviors applicable towards certain outcomes are assessed. Beliefs about many behaviors (including self-efficacy assessments, goal-outcome correlations, and possible impediments) influence the determination of the most favorable course to pursue (i.e., a positive attitude toward a specific behavior) that is motivated by expected outcomes. When self-directed learning activities are chosen to obtain desirable outcomes, as opposed to other nonlearning courses of action, the individual is theorized as having learner self-directedness. The manifestation of this self-directedness is participation in a self-directed learning activity that is comprised of wishes and intentions to engage in the self-directed learning activity, actual participation in the activity, and an evaluation of the actual outcomes resulting from participation. Self-directedness, or the propensity to engage in self-directed learning activities, is fostered when the correlation between actual and desired outcomes is great, and the agent comes to the realization that many desirable outcomes in life can result from independent learning processes.

From (Chapter 1) Figure 2, self-directed learning is a conative and behavioral process; that is, it represents what the learner intends to do and actually does with respect to the chosen learning activity. As such, self-directed learning is an intentional action that is comprised of all activities necessary to reach desired outcomes. Consistent with interactive emergent agency, this model of self-directed learning characterizes an activity in which agents (i.e., learners) are internally motivated to engage in based upon values and assessments of capability that are socially influenced and personally evaluated.

Autonomous Learning

Autonomous learning refers to a subset of the agentic actions performed by a learner in a self-directed learning project; that is, as compared to self-directed learning, autonomous learning is a less restrictive categorization that includes more varied types of learning activities. Activities related to resourcefulness (Carr, 1999), initiative (Ponton, 1999), and persistence (Derrick, 2001) form the core of autonomous learning. Following the conative analogy, an autonomous learner *shows* resourcefulness, initiative, and persistence in his or her self-directed learning activity.

Attending to the cognitive activities that comprise autonomous learning are essential to comprehend fully the notion of self-directed learning. The socially imposed concept of self-directed learning as learning that occurs in isolation does not reflect its essence. As asserted by Long (1989), psychological constructs are necessary in defining self-directed learning. A subset of these constructs is associated with autonomous learning. Consider a situation in which two individuals are involved in academic study. One studies to satisfy imposed requirements, course requirements for example, whereas the other studies to satisfy personal interests. On the surface, both learners are engaged in the same activity. If self-directed learning were identified solely upon these observable behaviors, then both individuals would merit self-directed learner status. However, if factors associated with autonomous learning were considered, the differences between the two learners and their activities would emerge.

The concept of learner resourcefulness as applied to autonomous learning is based upon Rosenbaum's (1989) nonautomatic self-control theory that addresses an agent's actions in responding to a stressful situation. Rosenbaum asserted that an agent faced with a stressful situation may opt to exercise redressive self-control by escaping the situation to one more comfortable. Alternatively, the agent may exercise reformative self-control by enduring the situational discomfort to reach long-term benefits. Reformative self-control involves skills which enable an individual, or agent, to manage short-term discomfort in order to engage in life altering activities. These skills include the individual's ability to anticipate future rewards, prioritize values, delay immediate gratification, and solve problems. Learning is a life altering activity. Self-directed learning activities induce stress as a consequence of learning requirements as well as having to manage them amidst life's other requirements.

Employing the skills associated with reformative self-control, Carr (1999) developed the construct of learner resourcefulness as it pertains to autonomous learning. In Carr's model, autonomous learner resourcefulness hinges on the learner's capacity to anticipate future rewards of present learning, prioritize learning over nonlearning activities, select learning over nonlearning activities, and resolve problems relative to the selected activity. However, Carr's model does not make the distinction between redressive and reformative self-control in that redressive self-control occurs for the sake of activity avoidance to invoke immediate gratification; Carr recognized that engagement in autonomous learning may be immediately gratifying for the learner in addition to leading to future benefits.

Ponton (1999) developed the five factor construct of personal initiative in autonomous learning based primarily upon research in business (Frese, Kring, Soose, & Zempel, 1996; Frohman, 1997; Ghiselli, 1971). The factors include goal-directedness, an active approach to problem solving, action-orientation, persistence in overcoming obstacles, and self-startedness. Goal-directedness refers to creating and working toward the accomplishment of personal learning goals. An active approach to problem solving is taking the responsibility to create solutions to impediments that interfere with one's learning. When an intention is created, a rapid transition from intention to behavior is action-orientation; thus, a learner displays action orientation when learning goals and plans are quickly enacted. Persistence in overcoming obstacles refers to the dogged pursuit of learning in spite of barriers. Finally, self-startedness describes learning that commences without the need of others.

The three factor construct of persistence is comprised of goal-directedness, self-regulation, and volition (Derrick, 2001). The goal-directedness factor differs from that defined by Ponton (1999) in that the focus is on perseverant action directed toward goal completion rather than working toward goals with characteristics that provide maximum motivation (i.e., goal specificity, challenge, and proximity; cf. Bandura, 1997; Locke & Latham, 1990). Self-regulation encompasses personal management strategies that enable persistent behavior. Volition refers to postdecisional motivation that represents the cognitive strategies enlisted after one decides on a course to pursue; other forms of cognitive motivation are predecisional in that they lead to the creation of an intention whereas volition motivates behavior *after* the intention is created.

Autonomous learning represents a set of cognitive activities that are enacted to varying degrees during self-directed learning tasks. Although not overt behavior in the traditional sense, resourcefulness, initiative, and persistence are made observable via valid instrumentation (cf. Carr, 1999; Derrick, 2001; Ponton, 1999). Consistent with SCT, the current conceptualization of autonomous learning recognizes the important role of these cognitive activities in agentic learning.

Autonomous Learning from a SCT Perspective

Autonomous learning is purposeful, intentional learning. Throughout the course of a single day, humans become aware of new information that is either purposefully sought or fortuitously realized; however, autonomous learning refers to the former. For example, while driving to a destination, one may notice and remember a new store. Because the purpose of the drive does not concern learning locations to new stores, this learning would not represent autonomous learning. However, if learning about the surroundings is the intent of the trip, then the drive is considered an autonomous learning activity in which learner initiative, resourcefulness, and persistence are manifest.

Human thought can influence action. Though incapable of initiating sophisticated environmental interactions, infants have the capacity to symbolize, reflect upon environmental stimuli, and learn vicariously. As physiological skills develop, the child acquires the capacity to use forethought in order to select activities with associated consequences that guide self-regulation. When the basis for selecting an activity is to learn specific content, the child engages in autonomous learning. Cognitive and affective factors provide the impetus for autonomous learning, the consequences of which provide the child with new information with which to influence future behavior.

Humans think and live in an objective reality that supplies information subject to individual interpretations. Though incomplete information may be known and incorrect logic used, humans decide which courses of action to pursue in light of perceived abilities and anticipated valued consequences. Expectations regarding valued consequences are derived from interpretations of past experiences, observations of others, or interaction between the two.

Through symbolization, beliefs about autonomous learning activities are cognitively considered particularly in relation to other activities. As illustrated in (Chapter 1) Figure 2, many activities are considered with respect to their perceived correlation to desirable outcomes. However, learner autonomy, like learner self-directedness, is presumed to exist when an agent is inclined to engage in autonomous learning activities to acquire desirable outcomes; that is, the agent has a favorable attitude toward autonomous learning activities. This favorable attitude may be based upon learning from others the value of autonomous learning or from past successful learning endeavors initially modeled by competent learners.

Even though an agent believes autonomous learning may lead to valued outcomes, pursuit of this course of action will not commence unless self-efficacy is present. For example, it is not enough for a person to correlate a college diploma in engineering with career opportunities and financial security to catalyze participation in such an undergraduate course of study; the agent must believe that capability is present to perform successfully the requisite scientific and mathematical coursework and persevere in a multiyear academic endeavor. Therefore, a person will not engage in autonomous learning unless both valued outcomes are anticipated and perceived capabilities are present.

Autonomous learning, then, represents learning that is not necessarily coincident with social isolation. The relevant self-efficacy assessment is whether or not an individual believes that capability is present to show initiative, resourcefulness, and persistence in a chosen learning activity. If the agent believes that a college course is an appropriate resource to accomplish some level of satisfaction and subsequently registers and participates in the course, then this activity is consistent with the concept of autonomous learning. Autonomous learning relates to the interactive emergent form of agency that recognizes the interactional influences among person, environment, and behavior. Therefore, social isolation is not a defining characteristic of autonomous learning.

Recent and Future Research on Autonomous Learning

Using data from a nonprobability sample of 909 adults, Ponton, Carr, et al. (2004) developed a path analytic model for autonomous learning and argued that persistence is heavily influenced by resourcefulness mediated by initiative. Thus, to foster autonomous learning tendencies, a learning facilitator should focus initial efforts on creating learner resourcefulness. When the facilitator helps learners to anticipate the future rewards of learning activities as opposed to nonlearning activities, learners prioritize and select learning over nonlearning activities.

Facilitators who create courses that provide opportunities for learners to develop academic skills and create assessments that highlight increases in learning capabilities equip the learner with the capacity, both actual and perceived, to solve the problems that interfere with desired levels of learning. Facilitators foster initiative when they help learners to create performance goals that are specific, challenging, proximal, and correlated to anticipated future rewards (i.e., desirable outcomes). Furthermore, fostering personal initiative encourages the development of a high level of personal responsibility not only to solve the problems associated with one's learning but also to create goals, plan learning activities, and persevere to personal levels of success. Persistence, as volition, results when valued goals are created and pursued, learning outcomes are monitored for desired levels of learning, and activities are modified to accomplish these goals and standards. Facilitators should create opportunities for autonomous learning in their courses and help students to value such learning as they develop efficacy in these conative factors.

To further investigate the path analytic relationship between resourcefulness and persistence, Ponton et al. (2005) conducted a follow up study using data from 492 adults. The results of this study suggest that while adults may anticipate the future rewards of learning, prioritize learning over nonlearning activities, and intend to show persistence in their learning, they may not actually choose learning over nonlearning activities. Ponton et al. (2005) argued that activity selection may be related to the many choices that busy adults have and that personal learning may be postponed due to the perceived exigencies of multiple life roles. Thus, to foster autonomous learning, a facilitator should prescribe methods (e.g., reflective journals) that help learners to assess the costs versus the benefits of activity choices. In this manner, the learner increases self-monitoring tendencies and is better able to invest time in activities that have long term value.

As self-efficacy plays an important role in instigating autonomous learning, Ponton, Derrick, et al. (2004) developed the Appraisal of Learner Autonomy (ALA) to measure self-efficacy in adult autonomous learning. The instrument was developed utilizing Bandura's (2001) guidelines in both scale creation and validation assessment. In light of the mediating role of self-efficacy in cognitive motivation, research using the ALA will be directed at confirming the role of self-efficacy as a predictor of the autonomous learning conates. Provided the model is supported, using the sources of efficacy information to guide the promotion of learner autonomy is tenable.

Concluding Remarks

Autonomous learning represents an intentional activity in which learning is pursued based upon individual preferences. Supported by motivation and self-efficacy, the exhibition of resourcefulness, initiative, and persistence in one's learning defines autonomous learning. When a person is inclined to engage in autonomous learning activities, even when other courses of action may lead to equally satisfying outcomes, the person is characterized as having learner autonomy. Thus, learner autonomy represents cognitive and affective processes that lead to the conative factors of autonomous learning.

Consistent with SCT, humans choose to engage in autonomous learning based upon an ideation of potential future states. Anticipating valued outcomes, formulating learning goals, planning learning activities, and monitoring the feedback from such activities, thereby influencing the self-regulation of continued action, is consistent with conceptions of both SCT and autonomous learning. These cognitive processes occur in a dynamic model that recognizes the bidirectional influence among three constituent factors: the environment, person, and behavior. Thus, autonomous learners as agents are not only influenced by the environment and their behaviors but they also influence the environment and their behaviors through purposeful action.

For many years, self-directed learning has been fluidic in definition. As a result, several researchers have attempted to focus instead on autonomous learning by creating a theoretical definition consistent with the current concepts of human behavior such as SCT. It is in this spirit that these researchers (cf. Carr, 1999; Derrick, 2001; Ponton, 1999) have attempted to not only provide a fresh line of inquiry but also to direct ongoing studies that better enable learning facilitators to foster learner autonomy among students. With continued studies directed toward the conative factors described in this chapter and other relevant constructs (e.g., curiosity, personal responsibility, self-efficacy), the facilitation of autonomous learning tendencies based on empirical evidence may be realized in just a few years. Accepting autonomous learning as an agentic activity consistent with SCT provides a heuristic framework that will continue to guide research and inform practice in facilitating lifelong learning and human empowerment through intentional development.

References

Ajzen, I. (2002). Perceived behavioral control, self-efficacy, locus of control, and the Theory of Planned Behavior. *Journal of Applied Social Psychology, 32*, 1-20.

Atkinson, J. W. (1964). *An introduction to motivation.* Princeton, NJ: D. Van Nostrand.

Bandura, A. (1986). *Social foundations of thought and action: A social cognitive theory.* Englewood Cliffs, NJ: Prentice Hall.

Bandura, A. (1989). Human agency in social cognitive theory. *American Psychologist, 44*(9), 1175-1184.

Bandura, A. (1997). *Self-efficacy: The exercise of control.* New York, NY: W. H. Freeman and Company.

Bandura, A. (2001). *Guide for constructing self-efficacy scales.* Unpublished manuscript, Department of Psychology, Stanford University, Stanford, CA.

Blankenship, V. (1985). The dynamics of intention. In M. Frese & J. Sabini (Eds.), *Goal directed behavior: The concept of action in psychology* (pp. 161-170). Hillsdale, NJ: Lawrence Erlbaum Associates.

Bugelski, B. R. (1964). *The psychology of learning applied to teaching.* Indianapolis, IN: Bobbs-Merrill.

Carr, P. B. (1999). *The measurement of resourcefulness intentions in the adult autonomous learner* (Unpublished doctoral dissertation). The George Washington University, Washington, DC.

Confessore, G. J. (1991). Human behavior as a construct for assessing Guglielmino's Self-Directed Learning Readiness Scale: Pragmatism revisited. In H. B. Long & Associates (Eds.), *Self-directed learning: Consensus & conflict* (pp. 123-146). Norman, OK: Oklahoma Research Center for Continuing Professional and Higher Education of the University of Oklahoma.

Derrick, M. G. (2001). *The measurement of an adult's intention to exhibit persistence in autonomous learning* (Unpublished doctoral dissertation). The George Washington University, Washington, DC.

Fishbein, M., & Ajzen, I. (1975). *Belief, attitude, intention, and behavior: An introduction to theory and research.* Reading, MA: Addison-Wesley.

Frese, M., Kring, W., Soose, A., & Zempel, J. (1996). Personal initiative at work: Differences between East and West Germany. *Academy of Management Journal, 39*(2), 37-63.

Frese, M., & Sabini, J. (1985). *Goal directed behavior: The concept of action in psychology.* Hillsdale, NJ: Lawrence Erlbaum Associates.

Frohman, A. L. (1997). Igniting organizational change from below: The power of personal initiative. *Organizational Dynamics, 25*(3), 39-53.

Ghiselli, E. E. (1971). *Explorations in managerial talent.* Pacific Palisades, CA: Goodyear.

Locke, E. A., & Latham, G. P. (1990). *A theory of goal setting & task performance.* Englewood Cliffs, NJ: Prentice Hall.

Long, H. B. (1989). Self-directed learning: Emerging theory and practice. In H. B. Long & Associates (Eds.), *Self-directed learning: Emerging theory & practice* (pp. 1-11). Norman, OK: Oklahoma Research Center for Continuing Professional and Higher Education of the University of Oklahoma.

Meyer, D. T. (2001). *The measurement of intentional behavior as a prerequisite to autonomous learning* (Unpublished doctoral dissertation). The George Washington University, Washington, DC.

Ponton, M. K. (1999). *The measurement of an adult's intention to exhibit personal initiative in autonomous learning* (Unpublished doctoral dissertation). The George Washington University, Washington, DC.

Ponton, M. K., & Carr, P. B. (1999). *A quasi-linear behavioral model and an application to self-directed learning* (NASA Technical Memorandum 209094). Hampton, VA: NASA Langley Research Center. **[cf. Chapter 1]**

Ponton, M. K., & Carr, P. B. (2000). Understanding and promoting autonomy in self-directed learning. *Current Research in Social Psychology, 5*(19). Retrieved from http://www.uiowa.edu/crisp/ **[cf. Chapter 2]**

Ponton, M. K., Carr, P. B., & Derrick, M. G. (2004). A path analysis of the conative factors associated with autonomous learning. *International Journal of Self-directed Learning, 1*(1), 59-69. **[cf. Chapter 8]**

Ponton, M. K., Derrick, M. G., Carr, P. B., & Hall, J. M. (2004, February). *The relationship between self-efficacy and autonomous learning.* Paper presented at the 18th International Self-Directed Learning Symposium, Cocoa Beach, FL. **[cf. Chapter 12]**

Ponton, M. K., Derrick, M. G., & Carr, P. B. (2005). The relationship between resourcefulness and persistence in adult autonomous learning. *Adult Education Quarterly, 55*(2), 116- 128. **[cf. Chapter 9]**

Rosenbaum, M. (1989). Self-control under stress: The role of learned resourcefulness. *Advances in Behaviour Research and Therapy, 11,* 249-258.

Vroom, V. H. (1964). *Work and motivation.* New York, NY: John Wiley and Sons.

Weiner, B. (1985). An attributional theory of achievement motivation and emotion. *Psychological Review, 92*(4), 548-573.

CHAPTER 4

AN AGENTIC PERSPECTIVE CONTRASTING AUTONOMOUS LEARNING WITH SELF-DIRECTED LEARNING[4]

Recent research has focused on autonomous learning without offering a clear differentiation between this construct and self-directed learning (SDL). The purpose of this chapter is to provide a heuristic position that suggests autonomous learning can be manifest in all three modes of agency (i.e., individual, proxy, or collective; Bandura, 2006) in the activation of learning activities; however, self-directed learning represents the degree to which personal agency is exercised individually by directing the creation of such activities. Thus, autonomous learning represents a necessary but not sufficient condition for SDL.

Over the past 10 years, several theorists (Ponton, 1999; Ponton & Carr, 1999, 2000; Ponton, Derrick, & Carr, 2005; Ponton & Rhea, 2006) have used the concept of agency to define autonomous learning. In this conceptualization, autonomous learning is viewed as an intentional manifestation of resourcefulness (Carr, 1999), initiative (Ponton, 1999), and persistence (Derrick, 2001) in learning activities based upon pre-existing desire (Meyer, 2001). Consistent with social cognitive theory (SCT; Bandura, 1986), the exhibition of such agency in one's learning is dependent upon the reciprocal interplay between person, environment, and behavior (i.e., reciprocal determinism); thus, the emergent interactive view of agency (Bandura, 1989) is the relevant conceptualization as opposed to mechanical or autonomous agency.

The theoretical placement of autonomous learning within the larger framework of self-directed learning (SDL) has lacked formal treatment using agency theory. While Ponton and Rhea (2006) theorized that autonomous learning represents a subset of actions within the quasi-

---

linear behavioral model of SDL first presented by Ponton and Carr in 1999, they were not explicit in their contrast of autonomous versus self-directed learning.

The purpose of this chapter is to provide a heuristic position that suggests autonomous learning can be manifest in all three modes of agency (i.e., individual, proxy, or collective; Bandura, 2006) in the activation of learning activities; however, self-directed learning represents the degree to which personal agency is exercised individually by directing the creation of such activities. Thus, autonomous learning represents a necessary but insufficient condition for SDL. Consistent with SCT, the important role of self-efficacy in personal agency will also be discussed as well as methods for its development using the individual agentic perspective to foster self-directedness.

Autonomous Learning and Agency

In 1999, Ponton defined autonomous learning as follows: "an agenti[c] learning process in which the conative factors of desire, initiative, resourcefulness, and persistence are manifest" (p. xiii). The importance of these four factors was first proposed by Confessore (1991). In this early work, Ponton simply defined agency as referring to "acts done intentionally" (p. xiii). In addition, he asserted the following:

> The difference between autonomous learning and self-directed learning is that autonomous learning represents a subset of activities [i.e., agentic actions] that can be associated with the process of self-directed learning. This subset of activities is the direct result of the learner's autonomy. (Ponton, 1999, p. 14)

This differentiation was made due to the focus of the working definition of autonomous learning on desire, resourcefulness, initiative, and persistence with an assumption that SDL would encompass many more learning processes. Since that time, the Learner Autonomy Profile (licensed to Human Resource Development Enterprises) has been used to assess learner autonomy by incorporating measures of desire (Meyer, 2001), resourcefulness (Carr, 1999), initiative (Ponton, 1999), and persistence (Derrick, 2001). More recently, a fifth instrument measuring self-efficacy in autonomous learning (Ponton, Derrick, Hall, Rhea, & Carr, 2005) has been added to the profile. As Ponton (1999) argued, the agentic perspective of autonomous learning was an explicit focus on Long's (1989) "psychological conceptualization" (p. 9) of self-directed learning as opposed to process perspectives of SDL.

The importance of defining autonomous learning as an agentic process is rooted in the notion that it is "purposeful, intentional learning" (Ponton & Rhea, 2006, p. 45) directed toward accomplishing learning goals of personal value. When one feels that a learning activity is a viable means to accomplish a valued outcome; perceives requisite ability to engage successfully in such an endeavor; and shows desire, initiative, resourcefulness, and persistence in such a learning activity one is engaging in an autonomous learning activity. However, such autonomy does not mean acting in isolation of environmental influences on thinking and action. Autonomous learning, like all other forms of human functioning, is dependent upon the bidirectional interaction between agent, environment, and behavior (see triadic reciprocal causation in Bandura, 1986). As learning generally involves the learner interacting with select learning resources, reciprocal determinism is explicitly relevant.

Social cognitive theory (Bandura, 1986) recognizes three models of agency: mechanical, autonomous, and emergent interactive (Bandura, 1989). Mechanical agency describes the unidirectional influence of the environment on behavior (i.e., radical behaviorism) whereas autonomous agency posits that thinking is the sole determinant of behavior independent of environmental influence (i.e., radical cognitivism); however, neither model of agency is consistent with SCT or current concepts of autonomous learning (Ponton & Rhea, 2006). Rather it is the third conceptualization of agency, emergent interactive, that recognizes the bidirectional interaction of all three factors— environment, person, and behavior—in determining emergent human functioning that is adopted by Bandura (1986, 1989) and Ponton and Carr (1999). In this model of agency, the person encompasses cognitive, affective, conative, and biological processes while the environment represents everything external to the agent.

Because of the bidirectional interaction modeled by reciprocal determinism, the environment can take three forms: imposed, selected, and created (Bandura, 1997). There are aspects of our physical and social surroundings that are imposed upon us regardless of our desires; however, even this imposition is still influenced by our cognitive appraisals and conative reactions. In addition, the environment represents a potentiality from which we purposely select aspects with which to engage thereby creating an actual environment. Finally, humans have the capability to create environments that would not otherwise exist. As is evident in these three environmental forms, humans play an important agentic role in construing, determining, and creating actual environments that correspond to increases in personal agency (Bandura, 1997).

There are no inconsistencies between autonomous learning as presently defined and manifest learning activities that involve all three forms of the environment. The learner who is autonomous can intentionally and proactively (a) engage in a learning activity by making sense of an imposed environment; (b) select an aspect of the potential environment, such as taking a course, to facilitate desired learning; or (c) direct the creation of a new learning activity that would not otherwise exist. Desire, resourcefulness, initiative, and persistence can be present in all three learning situations.

Note that even directing the creation of a new learning activity can involve resources created by others; "there is no absolute agency" (Bandura, 2006, p. 164). However, environmental creation should involve the reshaping of a situation into something new. In the case of learning, the transformation involves the creation of a learning activity that corresponds to the traditional self-regulatory/self-directed processes of self-evaluation, goal setting, planning, monitoring progress, and making process adjustments (cf. Knowles, 1975; Oddi, 1987; Zimmerman, Bonner, & Kovach, 1996; Zimmerman & Cleary, 2006).

There is a difference between personal agency and the modes through which this agency is exercised. Personal agency is exercised whenever one engages in the following: intentionality, forethought, self-regulation, and self-reflection (Bandura, 2006). These aspects of personal agency are evident in Ponton and Carr's (2000) description of autonomy in self-directed learning and their modeling of self-directed learning vis-à-vis learner self-directedness via the quasi-linear behavioral model (Ponton & Carr, 1999) based upon the work of Fishbein and Ajzen (1975). However, Bandura (2006) asserted that "everyday functioning requires an agentic blend" (p. 165) of the following three modes of personal agency: collective, proxy, and individual. Thus, personal agency is exercised through three distinct mechanisms.

Collective agency is exercised when one enlists a group of persons to synergistically contribute to the accomplishment of personally desired objectives. Proxy agency is realized when individuals influence "others who have the resources, knowledge, and means to act on their behalf to secure the outcomes they desire" (Bandura, 2006, p. 165). Finally, personal agency exercised individually describes the person who influences his or her thoughts, behaviors, and environment without relying on others. However, in all three modes of agency, personal agency is still manifest as long as the agent intentionally catalyzes action with the assistance of others, without such assistance, or using others as a proxy for personal functioning in an effort to accomplish anticipated outcomes while regulating personal thought and action with subsequent reflection upon the consequences of this manifest agency.

When a learning activity is construed as an environmental determinant that facilitates desired levels of learning, learner autonomy is present whether or not the varied forms of the environment (i.e., imposed, selected, or created) are activated by group, proxy, or individual, provided such activation occurs via personal agency. That is, a learner acts autonomously when he or she intentionally decides to choose the type of learning activity in which to engage. Such an activity can be (a) created solely by another (e.g., selecting a course that uses proxy agency for the instructional design), (b) created in concert with others (e.g., selecting/creating a group activity that uses collective agency to shape the activity), (c) created individually where the agent regulates every aspect of the activity, or (d) imposed upon the individual who then chooses to engage in sense-making; however, in all situations it is the autonomous learner who intentionally catalyzes individual learning due to personal desire, resourcefulness, initiative, and persistence.

Autonomous Learning Versus Self-Directed Learning

As mentioned earlier, Ponton (1999) stated the following:

> The difference between autonomous learning and self-directed learning is that autonomous learning represents a subset of activities that can be associated with the process of self-directed learning. This subset of activities is the direct result of the learner's autonomy. (p. 14)

The "subset of activities" refers to the agentic actions associated with resourcefulness, initiative, and persistence based upon the degree to which one believes himself or herself capable of acting intentionally (cf. "desire" with Meyer, 2001). Precursors to intention formulation also include motivation and self-efficacy (Ponton, Derrick, Confessore, & Rhea, 2005) and arguably personal responsibility (Ponton & Rhea, 2006). However, self-directed learning involves more than these psychological conceptualizations of action. Extant process models of self-regulation/self-directedness referenced in the previous section bring to the forefront important distinctions in the modes of agency through which self-directed learning is manifest when compared to autonomous learning.

Long (1989) asserted that SDL can be conceptualized along sociological (i.e., addressing learner isolation), pedagogical (i.e., addressing the learner's learning activities), or psychological (i.e., addressing the learner's mental activities) dimensions. Ponton (1999) asserted that the process description of SDL encompasses the sociological and pedagogical dimensions while the learner attribute description encompasses the construct of autonomy. Long stated the following:

> The psychological conceptualization implies that fundamentally learning is a self-initiated, self-directed, and self-regulated cognitive process whereby the learner can *choose* [emphasis added] to ignore instruction, to merely absorb it by casual attention, to carefully memorize without critical reflection, or to seek to change or create an understanding of information. (p. 9)

Long further asserted that only "the *psychological conceptualization* is both necessary and sufficient to explain SDL" (p. 10) thereby highlighting his position that agency, as emphasized by the importance of the learner's choice in the learning process itself, is the defining characteristic of SDL. It has already been argued that agency is the defining characteristic of autonomous learning; however, more recent propositions in agency theory suggest that perhaps the definition of SDL can and should be nuanced further.

A sole focus on the psychological dimension of the learner neglects important structural aspects of a self-regulated/self-directed learning activity. That is, a learning activity is a process that is purposely designed to accomplish a learning goal thereby resulting in a valued outcome (Ponton & Carr, 1999, 2000). Process descriptions congruent with the pedagogical dimension highlighted by Long (1989) are critical in understanding what is meant by self-directed learning as differentiated from autonomous learning. Autonomous learning focuses on the psychological dimension of the learner as manifest in certain cognitive based actions; however, it is presently proposed that self-directed learning involves these actions but much more: the creation of a learning environment through the individual mode of personal agency.

As argued earlier, personal agency in autonomous learning can be manifest in imposed, selected, or created learning environments and exercised via collective, proxy, or individual agency. In all combinations of these multiple dimensions a learner can show desire, initiative, resourcefulness, and persistence in his or her learning (e.g., when participating in a class); however, self-direction implies more action. Self-direction implies enlisting the self-regulatory processes of identifying discrepancies between current and desired states, planning learning activities with relevant resources to bridge this gap, monitoring progress to assess achievement, and providing corrective feedback to the learning activity; that is, the "directing" aspects of the learning activity. This is not an imposed or selected environment as much as it is one created by the individual. Thus, it is presently proposed that SDL represents the degree to which personal agency is exercised individually in the creation of a learning activity whereby autonomous learning represents a necessary but insufficient condition in defining SDL.

This differentiation between autonomous and self-directed learning does not preclude the notion that while participating in the former, the latter cannot exist. Exercising personal agency in any learning activity by incorporating self-directed learning would support an "agentic blend" (Bandura, 2006, p. 165) and influence eventual attainments. As an example, it is often the case that courses offered to students fully prescribe the required activities and resources. When an individual is motivated to learn and shows the resourcefulness, initiative, and persistence to intentionally enroll and fully engage in such a course, this participation becomes an exhibition of autonomous learning. However, if during the course the student realizes extant deficiencies exist, creates a plan to remedy discrepancies in knowledge or skills, participates in this individually created learning activity with self-selected resources, and monitors the adequacy of personal progress and the activity itself, self-directed learning is also occurring within this overall autonomous learning activity (i.e., the course itself). Achievement of personal goals often requires enlisting multiple modes of agency in an episodic manner.

A legitimate argument can be made that ambiguity exists when defining the creation of a learning activity particularly with respect to the planning and selection of resources. Following the example in the previous paragraph, should the "course" be viewed as a "self-selected resource" similar to a book in a library? If the conative factors associated with autonomous learning were exhibited in the intentional selection and study of a book where this could easily be defined as a self-directed learning activity based upon previous definitions, why would not enlisting personal agency to enroll in a course (albeit a different self-selected resource but a self-selected resource nonetheless) also be labeled SDL? The difference lies in the term "directed."

To direct learning not only involves an assessment of learning discrepancies and the creation of a learning activity by choosing appropriate resources and activities but also evaluating the adequacy of progress and the activity itself. In a self-directed learning activity, it is the self-reflective agent who decides whether or not desired levels of learning are achieved, not a proxy; in SDL, it is the self-regulatory agent who uses achievement feedback to modify the learning activity if desired levels of learning are not being achieved, not a proxy. Defining an activity as SDL requires the exhibition of personal agency via individual effort in all facets of the self-regulatory cycle.

Self-Efficacy Development

Bussey and Bandura (1999) stated the following:

> In the agentic sociocognitive view . . . people are self-organizing, proactive, self-reflective, and self-regulating, and not just reactive organisms shaped and shepherded by external events. The capacity to exercise control over one's thought processes, motivation, affect, and action operates through mechanisms of personal agency. Among the mechanisms of agency, none is more central or pervasive than people's beliefs in their capabilities to produce given levels of attainments. Unless people believe they can produce desired effects by their actions, they have little incentive to act or to persevere in the face of difficulties. Perceived efficacy is, therefore, the foundation of human agency. (p. 691)

The motivation to embark upon and persevere within a SDL activity requires the agent to believe that requisites skills are present to design and participate in such an activity in the face of impediments. "Perceived self-efficacy is conceptualized as *perceived operative capability*. It is concerned not with what one *has* [in terms of a repertoire of rudimentary behaviors] but with belief in what one *can do* with whatever resources one can muster" (Bandura, 2007, p. 646). Many impediments to self-efficacy in autonomous learning activities have already been argued and empirically supported as relevant for differentiating adult learners (Ponton, Derrick, Hall et al., 2005); these impediments should be equally relevant for SDL. However, due to the heuristic position presently proposed that SDL encompasses an expanded set of self-regulatory skills, self-efficacy development (and assessment) must go beyond mere agentic participation in a learning activity when it is not required by someone else (see Ponton, Derrick, Hall et al., p. 61) but must include facets of self-directing one's learning.

Self-efficacy appraisals are based upon four sources of information: enactive mastery experiences, verbal persuasion, vicarious experiences, and physiological/emotive arousals (Bandura, 1997). Capability is often perceived to exist when previous experiences have been successful and such successes are attributed to personal ability (i.e., mastery experience). In addition, when respected referents provide persuasive arguments to an individual that he or she is capable of a successful performance, the individual may begin to believe this is indeed the case (i.e., verbal persuasion). Individuals also appraise their respective capabilities by observing models deemed similar to themselves (i.e., vicarious experience). Finally, interpretations of physiological and affective arousals from participating in an enactive mastery experience can be interpreted as an indicant of incapability thereby weakening efficacy or as an indicant of expanding capability with a concomitant strengthening of efficacy beliefs. In all cases, it is the agent and not some external evaluator who reflects upon the varied forms of efficacy information and arrives at a resultant efficacy belief; self-efficacy is perceived capability developed subjectively through one's cognitive filters, not some objectified assessment of capability.

Within formal education, self-efficacy in SDL can be strengthened by attending to these sources of efficacy information. Mastery experiences in which students must act autonomously while directing all self-regulatory facets of a learning activity can be part of curricular requirements. Instructors can provide verbal persuasion to help convince students that resultant learning successes are attributable to personal capabilities rather than some outside facilitative influence (e.g., luck, assistance). Instructors can also highlight previously successful students as well as create group tasks that allow students to recognize the capabilities of similar others. Finally, instructors can help students to interpret arousals as indicants of expanding, rather than limited, capabilities. Armed with strong beliefs in personal efficacy, the self-directed learner is better able to reject disconfirming evidence of capability while selectively highlighting successful endeavors thereby feeling empowered to influence personal life trajectories via SDL activities.

Of course, this does not mean that humans whose self-efficacy in SDL was not intentionally attended to by outside agents are doomed to a life of dependency upon externally directed learning activities. The same sources of efficacy information are evaluated by all persons in or out of the classroom; thus, the development of self-efficacy is not confined to the walls of educational institutions. However, due to the resiliency of efficacy beliefs and the importance of preparing students for a lifetime of personal development, it should be a goal of formal education to attend to the development of self-directedness rather than leave it to happenstance after matriculation.

Concluding Remarks

The remarks presented are merely our perspective on autonomous learning and self-directed learning. Readers familiar with the SDL literature will find congruence between past ideas and those presented albeit with some variations in terminology. As constructs, the differentiation of autonomous with self-directed learning resides within the realm of human discussion and debate. However, as it has been our intent to remain as faithful as possible to the precepts of social cognitive theory as well as remain consistent in our definitions of terms, we felt it necessary to propose a position that differentiates autonomous learning from self-directed learning. In this manner, at least our writing can remain consistent with the theories upon which we stand.

In 1999, Ponton asserted that "self-directed learning exists without a unique definition" (p. 11) and cited Oddi (1987) and Merriam and Caffarella (1999) who observed that self-directed learning research can be dichotomized into two categories of perspectives: process or personality characteristic. The two perspectives, if viewed in isolation, can contribute to ambiguity in defining what constitutes SDL; however, the position of this chapter is that defining a learning activity as SDL involves attention to both perspectives with the added caveat that SDL learning activities are those in which the learner directs the creation of all associated self-regulatory processes thereby exercising personal agency individually. It is by adding this latter restriction that SDL can be differentiated from autonomous learning where the latter is a necessary but insufficient condition for defining SDL. Using agency theory, a unique definition for SDL is offered that we hope will spawn spirited debate.

References

Bandura, A. (1986). *Social foundations of thought and action: A social cognitive theory.* Englewood Cliffs, NJ: Prentice Hall.

Bandura, A. (1989). Human agency in social cognitive theory. *American Psychologist, 44*(9), 1175-1184.

Bandura, A. (1997). *Self-efficacy: The exercise of control.* New York, NY: W. H. Freeman and Company.

Bandura, A. (2006). Toward a psychology of human agency. *Perspectives on Psychological Science, 1*(2), 164-180.

Bandura, A. (2007). Much ado over a faulty conception of perceived self-efficacy grounded in faulty experimentation. *Journal of Social and Clinical Psychology, 26*(6), 641-658.

Bussey, K., & Bandura, A. (1999). Social cognitive theory of gender development and differentiation. *Psychological Review, 106*(4), 676-713.

Carr, P. B. (1999). *The measurement of resourcefulness intentions in the adult autonomous learner* (Unpublished doctoral dissertation). The George Washington University, Washington, DC.

Confessore, G. J. (1991). Human behavior as a construct for assessing Guglielmino's Self-Directed Learning Readiness Scale: Pragmatism revisited. In H. B. Long & Associates (Eds.), *Self-directed learning: Consensus & conflict* (pp. 123-146). Norman, OK: Oklahoma Research Center for Continuing Professional and Higher Education of the University of Oklahoma.

Derrick, M. G. (2001). *The measurement of an adult's intention to exhibit persistence in autonomous learning* (Unpublished doctoral dissertation). The George Washington University, Washington, DC.

Fishbein, M., & Ajzen, I. (1975). *Belief, attitude, intention, and behavior: An introduction to theory and research.* Reading, MA: Addison-Wesley.

Knowles, M. S. (1975). *Self-directed learning: A guide for learners and teachers.* Chicago, IL: Follett.

Long, H. B. (1989). Self-directed learning: Emerging theory and practice. In H. B. Long & Associates (Eds.), *Self-directed learning: Emerging theory & practice* (pp. 1-11). Norman, OK: Oklahoma Research Center for Continuing Professional and Higher Education of the University of Oklahoma.

Merriam, S. B., & Caffarella, R. S. (1999). *Learning in adulthood: A comprehensive guide* (2nd ed.). San Francisco, CA: Jossey-Bass.

Meyer, D. T. (2001). *The measurement of intentional behavior as a prerequisite to autonomous learning* (Unpublished doctoral dissertation). The George Washington University, Washington, DC.

Oddi, L. F. (1987). Perspectives on self-directed learning. *Adult Education Quarterly, 38*(1), 21-31.

Ponton, M. K. (1999). *The measurement of an adult's intention to exhibit personal initiative in autonomous learning* (Unpublished doctoral dissertation). The George Washington University, Washington, DC.

Ponton, M. K., & Carr, P. B. (1999). *A quasi-linear behavioral model and an application to self-directed learning* (NASA Technical Memorandum 209094). Hampton, VA: NASA Langley Research Center. [cf. Chapter 1]

Ponton, M. K., & Carr, P. B. (2000). Understanding and promoting autonomy in self-directed learning. *Current Research in Social Psychology, 5*(19). Retrieved from http://www.uiowa.edu/crisp/ [cf. Chapter 2]

Ponton, M. K., Derrick, M. G., & Carr, P. B. (2005). The relationship between resourcefulness and persistence in adult autonomous learning. *Adult Education Quarterly, 55*(2), 116-128. [cf. Chapter 9]

Ponton, M. K., Derrick, M. G., Confessore, G. J., & Rhea, N. E. (2005). The role of self-efficacy in autonomous learning. *International Journal of Self-Directed Learning, 2*(2), 81-90. [cf. Chapter 10]

Ponton, M. K., Derrick, M. G., Hall, J. M., Rhea, N. E., & Carr, P. B. (2005). The relationship between self-efficacy and autonomous learning: The development of new instrumentation. *International Journal of Self-Directed Learning, 2*(1), 50-61. [cf. Chapter 12]

Ponton, M. K., & Rhea, N. E. (2006). Autonomous learning from a social cognitive perspective. *New Horizons in Adult Education and Human Resource Development, 20*(2), 38-49. [cf. Chapter 3]

Zimmerman, B. J., & Cleary, T. J. (2006). Adolescents' development of personal agency: The role of self-efficacy beliefs and self-regulatory skill. In F. Pajares & T. Urdan (Eds.), *Self-efficacy beliefs of adolescents* (pp. 45-69). Greenwich, CT: Information Age.

Zimmerman, B. J., Bonner, S., & Kovach, R. (1996). *Developing self-regulated learners: Beyond achievement to self-efficacy.* Washington, DC: American Psychological Association.

CHAPTER 5

AN AGENTIC PERSPECTIVE OF SELF-DIRECTED LEARNING AS APPLIED TO CHILDREN[5]

Ponton (2009) presented an agentic perspective of self-directed learning (SDL) as contrasted to autonomous learning in order to provide a heuristic position by suggesting that whereas autonomous learning can be manifest in all three modes of agency (i.e., individual, proxy, or collective; Bandura, 2006b) in the activation of learning activities, SDL represents the degree to which personal agency is exercised individually. Ponton concluded that both the process and personality perspectives categorized by Oddi (1987) and Merriam and Caffarella (1999) are important to defining SDL and that SDL activities are those in which the learner individually directs the creation of associated self-regulatory processes as outlined by Zimmerman, Bonner, and Kovach (1996). Even though much of SDL research and theorizing rests within the domain of adult learning, the agentic perspective posited by Ponton is equally applicable to children.

The exercise of intentionality, or agency, in personal learning can occur at every age level provided the agent has developed sufficiently both physiologically and cognitively to proactively initiate interaction with the environment and engage in sense making. Ponton's (2009) notion of self-directed learning (SDL)—"the degree to which personal agency is exercised individually by directing the creation of . . . [learning] activities"—is thus equally applicable to children as it is to adults provided the former have developed sufficiently to exercise agentic learning. All of the associated constructs within a sociocognitive framework are salient in both understanding and facilitating self-directedness regardless of the learner's age.

However, this does not mean that the specific enactment of a child's self-directed learning is the same as for an adult. For children,

---

[5]This article is reprinted with permission from the *International Journal for Self-Directed Learning* (http://sdlglobal.com/journals.php) and is copyrighted © The International Society for Self-Directed Learning [2009, 6(1), 46-58]

(a) limited experiences provide limited information upon which to build percepts of personal capability for SDL (i.e., self-efficacy for SDL), (b) fewer personal resources create both situational and structural impediments to the exercise of self-directedness, (c) compulsory education provides experiences that can foster either self-directedness or dependence upon others for personal learning, and (d) requirements of a general education reduce opportunities to exercise personal agency in learning. Whereas the theoretical underpinnings of salient constructs are independent of age, developmental trajectories do influence how these constructs reveal themselves and impact the exercise of personal agency.

The purpose of this chapter is to offer an agentic perspective of self-directed learning for children. Using extant theories of agency (Bandura, 2006b) that include motivation and self-efficacy consistent with social cognitive theory (Bandura, 1986), this chapter will present a framework for understanding the occurrence of SDL among children as well as provide suggestions for the further development of SDL during formal or informal tuition. Part of the suggested facilitation process will be the role of autonomous learning as a mediating construct between dependent learning and SDL.

Social Cognitive Theory

Social Cognitive Theory (SCT; Bandura, 1986) posits an agentic view of human behavior in which intentional, purposeful action is guided by thought processes within the context of objective and subjective environments. This interactive notion of human functioning is referred to in SCT as triadic reciprocal causation and represents bidirectional influences between three constituent factors: person (i.e., biological, cognitive, affective, and conative aspects), behavior, and environment. This model of reciprocal determinism rejects radical notions of behaviorism and cognitivism that discount the role of thinking and the environment, respectively. (Note that "determinism" is used to describe a determining influence rather than an assurance of predictability.)

Thus, SCT adopts an emergent interactive view of personal agency rather than a mechanistic (i.e., behaviorist) or autonomous (i.e., cognitivist) perspective (Bandura, 1989) thereby describing human functioning as emerging from the following bidirectional interactions: (a) person/environment – people cognitively interpret the environment and create attitudes and conations with respect to environmental factors whereas the environment catalyzes internal thought processes by providing limitations and opportunities for personal agency, (b) person/behavior – internal personal factors drive behavior whereas the results of behavior provide feedback for self-reflection, and (c) behavior/environment – behaviors shape the environment whereas the environment provides an objective field in which to perform. Because of the explicit role of the person, human functioning cannot be predicted with certainty in a given scenario as it is dependent upon not only any objective facets of the situation but also the ideated, subjective context that is person and time dependent.

SCT recognizes the environment as taking three forms: imposed, selected, and created (Bandura, 1997). There are many aspects of our environment that are imposed upon us; however, this imposition can still be cognitively appraised thereby leading to the development of conative determinations. Additionally, the environment offers a multitude of potentialities from which individuals select facets thereby creating personal—and actual—environments. Finally, people can create environments that would not otherwise exist. Reciprocal determinism creates the opportunity for these three environmental forms—imposed, selected, and created—to exist and represent increases in personal agency (i.e., moving from an imposed to a created environment requires a greater degree of agency).

Humans are equipped with essential forms of cognitive functions that drive purposeful action (Bandura, 1986). By creating symbolic mental images, people can engage in forethought in which expectations of future events lead to the creation of goals and subsequent courses of action. Expectations of consequences and their correlations to individual activity are developed via vicarious learning and self-reflection of the results from previous personal action. Self-regulation is enlisted to reactively and proactively direct action toward desired ends.

Agency and Self-Efficacy

Personal agency refers to acts done intentionally and is exercised whenever one engages in the following: intentionality, forethought, self-regulation, and self-reflection (Bandura, 2006b). An agentic view of human functioning rejects the perspective of people as mere reactors to environmental inducements for action. Instead, humans are capable of purposeful, proactive, intentional action toward personally desired ends. Using forethought, people make appraisals as to which courses of action will lead to desirable outcomes and establish performance goals that correspond to these ends (cf. expectancy value theory and goal theory; Bandura, 1997). Thus, behaviors are enlisted intentionally to accomplish personal goals, and self-regulation is invoked to volitionally induce goal-directed action or modify courses of action when they are self-reflectively deemed as ineffective. As a means of sense making, self-reflection is the mechanism through which the agent cognitively interprets information that informs decision making and future courses of action.

There is a difference between personal agency and the manner in which it is exercised. Personal agency can be exercised in three various modes: collective, proxy, and individual (Bandura, 2006b). Collective agency is exercised when an individual enlists a group of others to work with the agent in support of personal performance goals. Proxy agency occurs when individual agents influence "others who have the resources, knowledge, and means to act on their behalf to secure the outcomes they desire" (Bandura, 2006b, p. 165). Lastly, personal agency exercised individually describes the situation in which the agent acts alone to accomplish personally satisfying ends. However, in all three modes of agency, personal agency is still exercised provided the agent proactively catalyzes action with or without the help of others or uses others to provide proxy action for personal functioning in support of accomplishing the agent's desired outcomes. Personal agency also encompasses self-regulatory thought and action with subsequent reflection used to scrutinize behavioral consequences.

A major determinant of the exercise of personal agency is one's perception of personal ability, which Bandura (1997) has termed self-efficacy. "Unless people believe they can produce desired effects by their actions, they have little incentive to act or to persevere in the face of difficulties. Perceived efficacy is, therefore, the foundation of human agency" (Bussey & Bandura, 1999, p. 691). It is the self-reflective capability of humans that determines the strength of efficacy beliefs as efficacy strength is based upon subjective appraisals from the following sources of information: mastery experiences, vicarious experiences, verbal persuasions, and physiological/emotive arousals. This information is used to make individual determinations of the degree to which one is capable of successfully executing a course of action in the face of impediments. "Perceived self-efficacy is conceptualized as *perceived operative capability*. It is concerned not with what one *has* [in terms of a repertoire of rudimentary skills] but with belief in what one *can do* with whatever resources one can muster [all italics in original]" (Bandura, 2007, p. 646).

Mastery experiences provide the most authentic indication of personal capability; that is, an agent should deem himself or herself capable of successfully executing a course of action when that same agent had previously done so in the past. Mastery experiences strengthen efficacy when previous successes are attributed to personal capability rather than to a facilitative environment (e.g., help from others). Individuals also appraise their capability by observing others deemed as similar to themselves (i.e., vicarious experiences); the greater the similarity, the greater the likelihood that observational modeling will strengthen efficacy beliefs. Verbal assurances of requisite capability from respected referents also provide persuasive indicants of personal ability (i.e., verbal persuasion). Finally, physiological and affective arousals from engaging in an activity can strengthen efficacy if subjectively associated with expanding capability or weaken efficacy if interpreted as a lack of capability. In these varied forms of efficacy information, it is the self-reflective agent who interprets the information thereby resulting in an individual determination of efficacy strength; self-efficacy is not an objective assessment of actual capability.

Autonomous Learning Vis-à-Vis SDL

In 1999, Ponton defined autonomous learning as "an agenti[c] learning process in which the conative factors of desire, initiative, resourcefulness, and persistence are manifest" (p. xiii). The term *agentic* is important because it recognizes autonomous learning as "purposeful, intentional learning" (Ponton & Rhea, 2006, p. 45) and a means to achieve personally satisfying ends. However, the focus of autonomous learning on desire, initiative, resourcefulness, and persistence limited its description to a "psychological conceptualization" (Long, 1989, p. 9) of learning. While such personality perspectives are important to the larger field of self-directed learning, Ponton (2009) asserted that SDL must also involve the process perspective consistent with Oddi (1987) and Merriam and Caffarella (1999). Ponton (2009) provided an argument that this is essential in not only differentiating autonomous learning from SDL but also in understanding the implications with respect to agency theory.

The autonomous learner can exhibit the conative factors of desire (Meyer, 2001), resourcefulness (Carr, 1999), initiative (Ponton, 1999), and persistence (Derrick, 2001) in all three environmental forms (i.e., imposed, selected, and created) recognized by SCT (Ponton, 2009).

That is, the autonomous learner can proactively and intentionally (a) engage in sense making from an imposed environment, (b) select an aspect of the environment (e.g., register for a course), or (c) create an entirely new learning activity to accomplish personal learning goals. Note that even the creation of a "new" learning activity can involve resources created by others ("there is no absolute agency"; Bandura, 2006b, p. 164); however, creating an environment should involve a distinct transformation into something that would not have otherwise existed. For a learning activity, this would involve all aspects of the traditionally defined self-regulatory (and self-directed) processes of self-evaluation (i.e., needs assessment), goal setting, planning, monitoring progress, and activity adjustments as necessary (cf. Knowles, 1975; Oddi, 1987; Zimmerman & Cleary, 2006; Zimmerman, Bonner, & Kovach, 1996).

However, the "creation" of a learning activity can be exercised through all three modes of personal agency (i.e., collective, proxy, and individual; Ponton, 2009). When an agent decides that a learning activity is needed in order to accomplish a desired outcome, the agent can (a) enlist the assistance of others to work collectively in the creation of an activity, (b) enlist the assistance of others to create an activity without the agent's assistance, or (c) create the activity individually without anyone's assistance. Ponton (2009) asserted that autonomous learning can be manifest through all modes of personal agency; however, SDL requires that the individual mode of agency be used to create/perform associated facets of the self-regulatory learning cycle.

Children Vis-à-Vis Adults

All humans—children or adults—can be described in a superordinate way via the same theories of behavior. Reciprocal determinism and personal agency do not become relevant at a particular age or stage of development. Even in the earliest months of existence, infants exert proxy agency when they proactively cry out for the efforts of others in their environment to satisfy personal needs (Choonara, 1999) and exert goal-directed personal agency when they select facets of the environment upon which to visually focus, cognitively appraise, and make behavioral adjustments (Butterworth, 1992; Meltzoff & Moore, 1997); research cited in Wellman and Gelman (1992) suggests that infants as young as 3-4 months can select anomalous facets of the environment upon which to focus extended attention. However, to assert that children are the same as adults would be a gross minimization of developmental processes. While value systems, efficacy appraisals, and impediments to proactivity exert their influences to both groups, nevertheless specific values, efficacy appraisals, and impediments to agency vary greatly by the accumulation of experiences and subsequent self-reflection through experientially dependent cognitive filters. Reciprocal determinism recognizes the salient interacting factors (i.e., person, environment, and behavior) to human functioning and the individualized, varied role of each.

"The newborn arrives without any sense of selfhood and personal agency" (Bandura, 2006b, p. 169). Because self-efficacy uses self-reflection to build its strength, limited experiences yield limited information upon which to build efficacy beliefs. Without mastery experiences, role models, persuasive encouragement from referents representing expert assessments, or somatic feedback interpreted from a growth perspective, a child has little reason to feel competent in particular courses of action. However, physiological development soon provides infants with the capability to transition from observers to producers of environmental happenings. When children interpret themselves as the cause of environmental changes, a sense of agency begins to develop (Bandura, 2006b). In time, the varied sources of efficacy information emerge and are used by the agent in fomenting efficacy appraisals. In fact, as efficacy beliefs are strengthened, disconfirming evidence of ability from additional experiences can even be cognitively discounted (Bandura, 1997).

Developmental trajectories require a consideration as to role of the changing self in social settings (Elder, 1994). All people—adults and children—engage in psychosocial interactions that affect the development and preservation of personal identity. However, children must also learn the rudiments of social interactions, manage hormonal changes with behavior in light of peer pressures, and scrutinize novel options (e.g., sex, drugs, and alcohol) with respect to an evolving personal value system interacting with social mores. The ability to successfully manage all of these situations and many more to achieve a healthy and productive lifestyle requires a strong sense of domain specific self-efficacy for overcoming structural and situational obstacles.

SDL and Children

With respect to structural obstacles to agentic learning, children have far fewer resources under their volitional control than do adults. A child generally does not have the option of (a) driving to—and perhaps paying for—a learning activity of personal interest, (b) spending all "free" time on personal learning as homework from compulsory education is required, and (c) deciding what to study in formal tuition because the curriculum of a general education permeates much of their education. Of course agency is certainly exercised when children—much to the chagrin of parents and teachers—pursue personal learning at the expense of learning mandated by adults.

The lack of personal resources at a child's disposal does limit the varied options to which self-directed learning can be manifest. That is, the exertion of personal agency to create a learning activity individually is affected by the subjective or objective resources at one's disposal. However, this does not mean that self-directed learning cannot occur in some form. For example, the child who decides to (a) learn about penguins (i.e., needs assessment), (b) read a book about penguins (i.e., goal setting), (c) pick a book from the bookshelf at home to read during the evening (i.e., planning), and (d) evaluate the level of personal satisfaction from the reading and decides whether or not to read a different book (i.e., activity adjustment) is engaging in self-directed learning. Reading the book is a learning activity that would not have otherwise existed had the child not created it intentionally, proactively, and individually. In addition, the activity would not reach a level of personal satisfaction had the child not evaluated the personal learning individually and exerted agency in modifying the activity as necessary.

SCT recognizes that self-inefficacy provides a psychological impediment to performance in addition to situational (e.g., illness) and structural obstacles (Bandura, 1997). The creation of a learning activity with an anticipated level of success requires the agent to believe that he or she is capable of doing so. As already mentioned, as compared to adults children have far fewer experiences regarding the manifestation of personally satisfying self-directed learning to base efficacy appraisals upon; therefore, their motivation to engage in self-directed learning is greatly diminished unless they believe they are able to exert such control to achieve desirable outcomes.

Development of SDL in Children

A neonate enters the world with a vast but unrealized ontogenetic potentiality to acquire knowledge and skills in all the varied trajectories that life can offer; that is, "a biological potentialist view [vs. a biological deterministic view] of human nature emphasizes human possibilities" (Bandura, 2001, p. 21). Even monozygotic twins become dissimilar with age due to unique interactions with individualized environments (McCartney, Bernieri, & Harris, 1990). In the beginning, infants are vastly limited in the degree to which they can exert personal agency in effecting their environments; however, research (cf. Leslie, 1987) has revealed that infants as young as 18 months have exerted personal agency in the individual creation of pretend play scenarios in which they purposefully are "acting as if" rather than "acting in error" in the use of available resources (Leslie, p. 413).

Like pretend play, self-directed learning can also emerge with little facilitation from others. However, the spectrum of activities that constitute "learning activities" varies greatly. As already posited, planning, choosing, enacting, and evaluating the learning from reading a single book on penguins is an exhibition of personal agency through the individual mode. Similarly, the planning, choosing, enacting, and evaluating the learning from reading a collection of books and articles on penguins, traveling to Antarctica to observe them, discerning the coincidence between what has been written and what is found experientially, and continuing this process until personal satisfaction is achieved is also "a" learning activity. Developing in children the cognitive and metacognitive processes (cf. Glaubman, Glaubman, & Ofir, 2001; Szente, 2007) to exert personal agency in self-directed learning and a sophisticated repertoire of potential learning strategies from which to choose enables them to exert proactive growth along chosen trajectories. Because children participate in compulsory education, society has the opportunity to facilitate development to this end. Bandura (2006a) asserted the following:

> A major goal of formal education is to equip students with the intellectual tools, self-beliefs, and self-regulatory capabilities to educate themselves throughout their lifetime. The rapid pace of technological change and accelerated growth of knowledge are placing a premium on capability for self-directed learning. (p. 10)

This should also be the goal of informal tuition outside of school.

Fostering self-directedness begins with fostering autonomy. Exhibiting desire, resourcefulness, initiative, and persistence in one's learning through all modes of personal agency is a necessary first step toward self-directed learning. For children, this initially means exhibiting the learner autonomy to seek out an adult's assistance and work collectively to learn something of personal value (i.e., collective agency). Later such autonomy is manifest when the child asks an adult to help him or her identify/gather a learning resource (i.e., proxy agency). Finally, the child exerts the highest form of agency in a manifest self-directed learning activity when he or she autonomously exerts personal agency in individually self-regulating associated facets of the learning activity from conceptualization through enactment to evaluation. Ponton and Carr (2000) discussed in detail the various facets of autonomy and methods of promotion to inform the development of autonomy in learning.

However, a child will not engage in either autonomous or self-directed learning unless requisite levels of efficacy exist. Such efficacy can exist at various levels of participation. For example, without a sense of collective efficacy a child will not seek out the help of others who the child feels are incapable of assistance. Thus, to promote collective efficacy and a willingness of the child to seek out assistance from a particular person (e.g., a parent) that person must attend to the four sources of efficacy information already discussed to facilitate the development of collective efficacy. That is, successful learning must be attributed to this particular group's effort, expressions of collective capability must be verbalized, an understanding that successful adult/child learning activities are typical of others, and stressors must be interpreted as indicants of an emergent group capability. When this occurs, the child is more likely to seek out this person for future collective learning due to a sense of collective efficacy.

Proxy efficacy is built in a similar manner. A child must believe that the proxy is capable of creating a satisfying learning activity. Such efficacy is built upon attending to the same sources of efficacy information but now conceptualized to the proxy mode of personal agency.

Self-efficacy is important whether personal agency in autonomous learning is exercised collectively or by proxy. A child must believe that requisite capability exists to enlist the help of others. It would be difficult to imagine asking someone for help when that person has been unwilling to provide any in the past. Therefore, to foster a child's self-efficacy for autonomous learning adults need to provide the level of assistance *requested* by the child. That is, the child's agency must be developed by the adult responding to the child's requests and not imposing learning activities beyond this.

At the highest level of personal agency in one's learning resides self-directed learning. It is at this stage of development that the agent believes requisite capability exists to *autonomously* (i.e., show desire, resourcefulness, initiative, and persistence) and *individually* create and regulate associated aspects of the learning activity. To foster self-efficacy for self-directed learning, children must be (a) provided opportunities to enact mastery experiences of the entire self-regulatory learning cycle at appropriate levels of challenge thereby strengthening beliefs in expanding personal capabilities, (b) persuaded by valued others that the capability to succeed in mastery experiences are present, (c) given successful models that highlight similarities thereby supporting the notion of "if that person like me can master this experience, I can to," and (d) guided in interpreting physiological or emotive arousals from enactive mastery experiences not as indicants of incapability but rather as natural responses to novel pursuits. While similar efficacy building strategies can and should be used for academic self-efficacy (cf. Margolis & McCabe, 2003), the focus of self-efficacy for SDL is with respect to an exertion of personal agency in learning through individual efforts; thus, mastery experiences should be provided accordingly (cf. Bandura & Schunk, 1981).

However, self-efficacy is not merely a possession of abilities but rather is a strength of assurance that successful execution can be performed in light of situational demands (Bandura, 2007; see also Ponton, Derrick, Hall, Rhea, & Carr, 2005, for an application of this principle to the measure of self-efficacy for autonomous learning). This brings to light the important construct of resourcefulness and its role in autonomous learning (Ponton, Carr, & Derrick, 2004; Ponton, Derrick, & Carr, 2005). Based upon the work of Rosenbaum (1989) regarding the repertoire of self-control skills needed to manage stressful situations, Carr (1999) conceptualized learner resourcefulness in a similar manner. Fostering self-efficacy for self-directed learning must include the development of the cognitive strategies associated with autonomous learning and not just the self-regulatory skills associated with process management.

Self-efficacy is a domain specific construct; therefore, one may not feel equally efficacious in engaging in self-directed learning for every conceivable topic of interest. Reciprocal determinism posits that personological factors will bidirectionally interact with both the real and imagined environment as well as with behaviors thereby leading to a development of the unique person; thus, no two people are identical in all domains of self-efficacy or any other constellation of psychological constructs. However, formal and informal tuition should work diligently to provide children with the opportunities to enhance their efficacy for self-directed learning by facilitating the pursuit of personal learning spawned by either compulsory education or outside interests. In this manner, children are empowered to leave formal education with the self-directedness to exert personal agency in fulfilling chosen aspirations via independent learning. Efforts to this end are not new (cf. Scardamalia & Bereiter, 1991) but must be pervasive and considered a worthwhile investment of the academic day; as Biemiller and Meichenbaum (1992) so aptly stated, "students might be exposed to fewer subjects [in school] but would be truly able to use what skills they have for purposes they value" (p. 79).

However, other benefits associated with a strong belief in academic and self-regulatory efficacy (i.e., perceived ability to master academic activities and self-regulate personal learning) are realized even before graduation. Based upon research, Bandura (1993) asserted the following:

> Children who have a high sense of academic and self-regulative efficacy behave more prosocially, are more popular, and experience less rejection by their peers than do children who believe they lack these forms of academic efficacy. . . . Moreover, a low sense of academic and self-regulatory efficacy is associated with emotional irascibility, physical and verbal aggression, and ready disengagement of moral self-sanctions from harmful conduct. (p. 138)

Thus the empowerment provided by a strong sense of personal efficacy for learning can manifest itself in the exercise of control over other important spheres of human functioning.

Children receive efficacy information from homes, schools, and other social environments (Schunk & Meece, 2006); thus, an important area of attention in the facilitation of self-efficacy for SDL in children is the self-efficacy of others to do so. Parents, teachers, and school staff must believe themselves capable of successfully creating facilitative opportunities for children to develop in this manner. This begins first by social change agents (e.g., policy makers) convincing these persons that self-efficacy for SDL is an important educational objective followed by the learning of efficacy building strategies with attention to the four sources of efficacy information. Without a strong sense of efficacy to create such environments, the motivation to do so will wane. Professionally trained educators may have to take a lead role in the education of parents in this regard.

Concluding Remarks

Just as with adults, children are capable of exerting personal agency in their various spheres of activities. It is the responsibility of adults to strengthen children's beliefs in their personal efficacy to exert agentic influence over their lives in positive, health promoting ways. Agentic learning should be included as a developmental focus as it is through such learning that an individual can decide how he or she wants to fulfill personal aspirations throughout the lifespan when the influence of childhood adults is diminished.

Building children's self-efficacy for SDL requires not only attention to process perspectives associated with the self-regulatory cycle of individually identifying needs, developing plans, proactively engaging in learning, evaluating feedback, and developing corrective strategies but also attention to the conative factors of desire, resourcefulness, initiative, and persistence. In addition, parents, teachers, and institutional staff must also possess the requisite efficacy to promote children's self-efficacy for SDL. Educational policy makers play a crucial role in providing the opportunity for all stakeholders to break the bonds of dependency on institutions for personal learning thereby permitting children to develop into adults who are empowered to enact personal change through self-directed learning.

References

Bandura, A. (1986). *Social foundations of thought and action: A social cognitive theory.* Englewood Cliffs, NJ: Prentice Hall.
Bandura, A. (1989). Human agency in social cognitive theory. *American Psychologist, 44*(9), 1175-1184.
Bandura, A. (1993). Perceived self-efficacy in cognitive development and functioning. *Educational Psychologist, 28*(2), 117-148.

Bandura, A. (1997). *Self-efficacy: The exercise of control.* New York, NY: W. H. Freeman and Company.

Bandura, A. (2001). Social cognitive theory: An agentic perspective. *Annual Review of Psychology, 52,* 1-26.

Bandura, A. (2006a). Adolescent development from an agentic perspective. In F. Pajares & T. Urdan (Eds.), *Self-efficacy beliefs of adolescents* (pp. 1-43). Greenwich, CT: Information Age.

Bandura, A. (2006b). Toward a psychology of human agency. *Perspectives on Psychological Science, 1*(2), 164-180.

Bandura, A. (2007). Much ado over a faulty conception of perceived self-efficacy grounded in faulty experimentation. *Journal of Social and Clinical Psychology, 26*(6), 641-658.

Bandura, A., & Schunk, D. H. (1981). Cultivating competence, self-efficacy, and intrinsic interest through proximal self-motivation. *Journal of Personality and Social Psychology, 41*(3), 586-598.

Biemiller, A., & Meichenbaum, D. (1992). The nature and nurture of the self-directed learner. *Educational Leadership, 50*(2), 75-80.

Bussey, K., & Bandura, A. (1999). Social cognitive theory of gender development and differentiation. *Psychological Review, 106*(4), 676-713.

Butterworth, G. (1992). Origins of self-perception in infancy. *Psychological Inquiry, 3*(2), 103-111.

Carr, P. B. (1999). *The measurement of resourcefulness intentions in the adult autonomous learner* (Unpublished doctoral dissertation). The George Washington University, Washington, DC.

Choonara, I. (1999). Why do babies cry? We still know too little about what will ease babies' pain. *British Medical Journal, 319,* 1381.

Derrick, M. G. (2001). *The measurement of an adult's intention to exhibit persistence in autonomous learning* (Unpublished doctoral dissertation). The George Washington University, Washington, DC.

Elder, G. H., Jr. (1994). Time, human agency, and social change: Perspectives on the life course. *Social Psychology Quarterly, 57*(1), 4-15.

Glaubman, R., Glaubman, H., & Ofir, L. (1997). Effects of self-directed learning, story comprehension, and self-questioning in kindergarten. *The Journal of Educational Research, 90*(6), 361-374.

Knowles, M. S. (1975). *Self-directed learning: A guide for learners and teachers.* Chicago, IL: Follett.

Leslie, A. M. (1987). Pretense and representation: The origins of "Theory of Mind." *Psychological Review, 94*(4), 412-426.

Long, H. B. (1989). Self-directed learning: Emerging theory and practice. In H. B. Long & Associates (Eds.), *Self-directed learning: Emerging theory & practice* (pp. 1-11). Norman, OK: Oklahoma Research Center for Continuing Professional and Higher Education of the University of Oklahoma.

Margolis, H., & McCabe, P. P. (2003). Self-efficacy: A key to improving the motivation of struggling learners. *Preventing School Failure, 47*(4), 162-169.

McCartney, K., Bernieri, F., & Harris, M. J. (1990). Growing up and growing apart: A developmental meta-analysis of twin studies. *Psychological Bulletin, 107*(2), 226-237.

Meltzoff, A. N., & Moore, M. K. (1997). Explaining facial imitation: A theoretical model. *Early Development and Parenting, 6*, 179-192.

Merriam, S. B., & Caffarella, R. S. (1999). *Learning in adulthood: A comprehensive guide* (2nd ed.). San Francisco, CA: Jossey-Bass.

Meyer, D. T. (2001). *The measurement of intentional behavior as a prerequisite to autonomous learning* (Unpublished doctoral dissertation). The George Washington University, Washington, DC.

Oddi, L. F. (1987). Perspectives on self-directed learning. *Adult Education Quarterly, 38*(1), 21-31.

Ponton, M. K. (1999). *The measurement of an adult's intention to exhibit personal initiative in autonomous learning* (Unpublished doctoral dissertation). The George Washington University, Washington, DC.

Ponton, M. K. (2009). An agentic perspective contrasting autonomous learning with self-directed learning. In M. G. Derrick & M. K. Ponton (Eds.), *Emerging directions in self-directed learning* (pp. 65-76). Chicago, IL: Discovery Association Publishing House. **[cf. Chapter 4]**

Ponton, M. K., & Carr, P. B. (2000). Understanding and promoting autonomy in self-directed learning. *Current Research in Social Psychology, 5*(19). Retrieved from http://www.uiowa.edu/crisp/ **[cf. Chapter 2]**

Ponton, M. K., Carr, P. B., & Derrick, M. G. (2004). A path analysis of the conative factors associated with autonomous learning. *International Journal of Self-Directed Learning, 1*(1), 59-69. **[cf. Chapter 8]**

Ponton, M. K., Derrick, M. G., & Carr, P. B. (2005). The relationship between resourcefulness and persistence in adult autonomous learning. *Adult Education Quarterly, 55*(2), 116-128. **[cf. Chapter 9]**

Ponton, M. K., Derrick, M. G., Hall, J. M., Rhea, N., & Carr, P. (2005). The relationship between self-efficacy and autonomous learning: The development of new instrumentation. *International Journal of Self-Directed Learning, 2*(1), 50-61. **[cf. Chapter 12]**

Ponton, M. K., & Rhea, N. E. (2006). Autonomous learning from a social cognitive perspective. *New Horizons in Adult Education and Human Resource Development, 20*(2), 38-49. **[cf. Chapter 3]**

Rosenbaum, M. (1989). Self-control under stress: The role of learned resourcefulness. *Advances in Behaviour Research and Therapy, 11,* 249-258.

Scardamalia, M., & Bereiter, C. (1991). Higher levels of agency for children in knowledge building: A challenge for the design of new knowledge media. *The Journal of the Learning Sciences, 1*(1), 37-68.

Schunk, D. H., & Meece, J. L. (2006). Self-efficacy development in adolescence. In F. Pajares & T. Urdan (Eds.), *Self-efficacy beliefs of adolescents* (pp. 71-96). Greenwich, CT: Information Age.

Szente, J. (2007). Empowering young children for success in school and in life. *Early Childhood Education Journal, 34*(6), 449-453.

Wellman, H. M., & Gellman, S. A. (1992). Cognitive development: Foundational theories of core domains. *Annual Review of Psychology, 43,* 337-375.

Zimmerman, B. J., & Cleary, T. J. (2006). Adolescents' development of personal agency: The role of self-efficacy beliefs and self-regulatory skill. In F. Pajares & T. Urdan (Eds.), *Self-efficacy beliefs of adolescents* (pp. 45-69). Greenwich, CT: Information Age.

Zimmerman, B. J., Bonner, S., & Kovach, R. (1996). *Developing self-regulated learners: Beyond achievement to self-efficacy.* Washington, DC: American Psychological Association.

CHAPTER 6

AUTONOMOUS LEARNING AND TRIADIC RECIPROCAL CAUSATION: A THEORETICAL DISCUSSION[6]

Essential to social cognitive theory is the notion of triadic reciprocal causation through which human functioning is understood by considering interactions between the person, behavior, and the environment. Due to the lack of a balanced discussion of autonomous learning through the lens of reciprocal determinism in the literature, the purpose of this chapter is to offer such a discussion that highlights how autonomous learning—like any domain of human functioning— can only be adequately understood by considering the reciprocity of interaction between the learner, his or her learning behaviors, and the environment.

Social cognitive theory (SCT; Bandura, 1986) supports an emergent interactive view of personal agency (Bandura, 1989) in which human functioning is described by the reciprocal interplay of three constituent factors—person, environment, and behavior—referred to as triadic reciprocal causation. Bandura (1986) asserted the following: "progress in understanding how personal factors affect actions and situations is best advanced through the microanalysis of interactive processes" (p. 28); therefore, understanding any domain of intentional action (i.e., personal agency) requires an analysis of not only these factors but also their interaction.

For more than 10 years, SCT has been used as a theoretical framework for developing new conceptualizations of autonomous learning as well as self-directed learning (cf. Ponton, 1999; Ponton, 2009; Ponton & Carr, 1999; Ponton & Carr, 2000; Ponton, Derrick, & Carr, 2005; Ponton & Rhea, 2006). Thus, triadic reciprocal causation (TRC) has been an explicit part of this emerging literature. Unfortunately, the use of the behavioral model of Fishbein and Ajzen

---

[6]This article is reprinted with permission from the *International Journal for Self-Directed Learning* (http://sdlglobal.com/journals.php) and is copyrighted © The International Society for Self-Directed Learning [2012, *9*(1), 1-10]

(1975; cf. Ponton & Carr, 1999) at various international meetings by these same theorists in order to describe the conative roles of desire (cf. Meyer, 2001), resourcefulness (Carr, 1999), initiative (Ponton, 1999), and persistence (Derrick, 2001) with respect to autonomous learning (cf. Confessore, 1991) has created a seeming overemphasis on the person-behavior interaction (i.e., learner autonomy vis-à-vis autonomous learning) at the expense of the other two (i.e., person-environment and behavior-environment interactions). The purpose of this chapter is to discuss all three interactions in greater detail and outline not only bidirectional influences but also mediating paths.

Background

Social cognitive theory supports an agentic view of human activity, portraying people as proactive, intentional initiators of their actions and thoughtful self-reflectors of associated consequences. Unlike earlier theories of psychology that either discount the role of thinking on action (i.e., radical behaviorism) or the environment on action (i.e., radical cognitivism), SCT recognizes that the exhibition of agency depends upon the reciprocal interplay of all three of the following determinants: person (cognitive, affective, conative, and biological aspects), behavior, and environment (Bandura, 1986). These interacting factors constitute a model referred to as triadic reciprocal causation (see Figure 1). These three factors influence each other bidirectionally and interact to varying degrees dependent upon temporal and situational factors that include subjective perceptions and objective environments. Thus, causation describes mutual influence rather than a certainty of outcome.

In 1999, Ponton defined autonomous learning as follows: "an agenti[c] learning process in which the conative factors of desire, initiative, resourcefulness, and persistence are manifest" (p. xiii); these four factors were proposed by Confessore in 1991 as salient to autonomous learning. Ponton (2009) later asserted that "personal agency in autonomous learning can be manifest in imposed, selected, or created learning environments and exercised via collective, proxy, or individual agency" (p. 70). As a manifestation of personal agency, the phenomenon of autonomous learning can only be adequately understood by an analysis of the interactions associated with the TRC model.

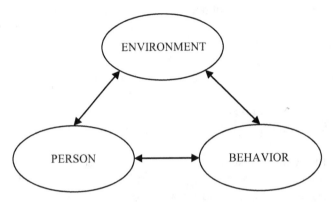

Figure 1. A model of the three interacting determinants used to describe human functioning (Bandura, 1986, p. 24).

The importance of using agency theory to understand autonomous learning is based upon the premise that autonomous learning refers to "purposeful, intentional learning" (Ponton & Rhea, 2006, p. 45) directed toward learning goals of personal value. Personal agency is exercised whenever one uses forethought to motivate and guide action, acts intentionally in activating plans, regulates action toward goal accomplishment, and reflects upon actions and consequences to both learn and motivate future action (cf. Bandura, 2006). The motivating dynamics associated with forethought are explained by expectancy value theory (Atkinson, 1964; Vroom, 1964) and goal theory (Locke & Latham, 1990); the dynamics associated with self-reflection are explained by attribution theory (Weiner, 1985). Thus, when a person believes that learning represents an appropriate path to obtain a valued outcome, establishes a learning plan and goal to reach this outcome, is motivated to engage in the plan and pursue the goal based upon perceived valence in relation to other desirable outcomes as well as perceived capability to be successful in the learning, and intentionally acts with manifest resourcefulness, initiative, and persistence, then one is engaging in an autonomous learning activity. Note that the "plan" can be deciding to pay attention to a facet of an imposed environment, select aspects of the environment that support learning, or create entirely new environments; however, agency requires such intentional forethought regardless of the plan's complexity. In addition, personal agency is exercised whether the learning activity is created by oneself (individual agency), by working with others (collective agency), or by someone else who the agent deems to have salient knowledge and skills (proxy agency) because it is the agent who intentionally acts regardless of the mode through which the agency is exercised (Bandura, 2006). (Note: In 2009, Ponton argued that *self-directed learning* occurs when the agent uses individual agency to create and direct learning activities in contrast to the multiple modes of agency and varied forms of the environment that can be used in autonomous learning.)

In 1999, Bussey and Bandura asserted the following:

> In the agentic sociocognitive view . . . people are self-organizing, proactive, self-reflective, and self-regulating, and not just reactive organisms shaped and shepherded by external events. The capacity to exercise control over one's thought processes, motivation, affect, and action operates through mechanisms of personal agency. Among the mechanisms of agency, none is more central or pervasive than people's beliefs in their capabilities to produce given levels of attainments. Unless people believe they can produce desired effects by their actions, they have little incentive to act or to persevere in the face of difficulties. Perceived efficacy is, therefore, the foundation of human agency. (p. 691)

Motivational considerations such as value expectancies and causal and effort attributions do not result in actual motivation to engage in a given activity unless beliefs in personal capability—i.e., self-efficacy—are strong (Bandura, 1997). In general, people do not choose to engage in perceived futile endeavors; therefore, preferential activities transform into chosen pursuits based upon a strong sense of efficacy.

Using the self-reflective capability of personal agency, self-efficacy is based upon appraisals of four sources of information: enactive mastery experiences, verbal persuasion, vicarious experiences, and physiological/emotive arousals (Bandura, 1997). The most authentic mechanism in building a strong sense of efficacy occurs when previous successful performances are personally attributed to ability rather than luck or the assistance from others (i.e., mastery experiences). Self-efficacy can also be strengthened when the valued opinions of others communicate to the agent that he or she has requisite capability (i.e., verbal persuasion). SCT also recognizes the power of observational learning particularly when personal experiences are lacking; therefore, people appraise their own capabilities by watching models deemed as similar (i.e., vicarious experiences) as suggested by the expression "if that person can do it, so can I." Finally, interpretations of somatic feedback can be used to strengthen efficacy provided such feedback is interpreted as a natural, epiphenomenal reaction based upon the task at hand or as a temporary indicant of expanding capability. Note that the locus of information associated with enactive mastery experiences and physiological/emotive arousals is behavior whereas the locus for verbal persuasion and vicarious experiences is the environment; however, it is the person who receives and interprets this information thereby formulating beliefs in personal efficacy.

The environment includes objective and subjective aspects and can be shaped dynamically or statically. The objective environment includes the people, natural and manmade structures, and social systems that surround us; the subjective environment includes how we perceive the world around us. Both environments influence how we think, feel, and behave and can either facilitate or impede desired courses of action. In addition, environments can be proactively created (i.e., dynamically shaped via intentional thought or action) or reactively realized (i.e., statically shaped as a response to who we are). In the latter case, the environment refers to the social environment that reacts to one's physical characteristics, status, or any other known characteristics; the environmental reaction occurs without purposeful causal action by the person (Bandura, 1986). A given person's social environment includes those people who have chosen to be part of this environment and to interact in a manner influenced by their understanding of this person.

Discussion

The literature presented provides many salient constructs related to human functioning in general and autonomous learning in particular. However, such functioning is the result of a dynamic interplay of the TRC determinants. SCT rejects the notion that any human activity can be understood by either focusing on any subset of these determinants (e.g., a study of only the person, environment, or behavior) or considering a subset of interactions. The development of a complete picture of autonomous learning requires a complete discussion of this interplay in light of the aforementioned constructs.

Direct Effects

With three determinants, the TRC model provides six direct effects (see Figure 2). Using the theoretical ideas presented, each direct effect can be described as follows:

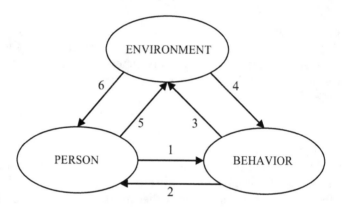

Figure 2. Six possible direct effects associated with the TRC model.

1. P → B:
Motivational considerations coupled with self-efficacy provide the motivation for the agent to engage in autonomous learning in pursuit of new knowledge or skills. Example: a person anticipates satisfaction from learning more about a particular topic (i.e., a motivational consideration), decides that requisite capability exists to learn about this topic via a particular learning activity (i.e., an efficacy appraisal), and participates in this learning activity.

2. B → P:
Autonomous learning leads to outcomes that inform motivational considerations as well as provides information (i.e., mastery experiences and physiological/emotive arousals) that informs efficacy beliefs; autonomous learning also leads to new knowledge or skills. Example: a person experiences a great deal of satisfaction from the learning associated with a learning activity (i.e., informs motivation) and believes that requisite capability to learn further from this activity is present (i.e., informs efficacy).

3. B→ E:
The autonomous learner focuses on aspects of an imposed environment or selects/creates an environment via individual, proxy, or collective agency conducive to autonomous learning. Example: a person selects a college course designed by a professor (i.e., a learning activity created via proxy agency).

4. E → B:
The environment either facilitates or impedes autonomous learning. Example: a tutor selected by a student helps the student to learn.

5. P → E:
Personal characteristics affect social environments (i.e., those persons, which include models and persuaders, who choose to surround the agent as well as the manner that they behave and the information that they convey). Example: a famous person enters a room filled with people and affects their behavior by his or her physical qualities and reputed characteristics.

6. E → P:
Social experiences influence values and expectations; events influence time and situationally dependent motivational considerations; verbal persuasion influence efficacy beliefs. Example: A lull in familial activities on a Saturday afternoon motivates a mother to engage in an hour of reading about a topic of interest (i.e., time and situationally dependent motivation).

Mediating Processes

An extension of the direct effects, six complete (i.e., full cycle associated with the TRC model) mediating processes can also be described:

1. P → E → B → P:
Personal characteristics affect social environments that can facilitate or impede autonomous learning thereby producing within the agent (a) outcomes that inform motivational considerations, (b) efficacy information, and (c) new knowledge or skills.

2. P $\rightarrow$ B $\rightarrow$ E $\rightarrow$ P:

The agent intentionally engages in autonomous learning via an environment conducive to learning. This learning activity, when observed, affects others who provide verbal persuasion that influence the agent's efficacy beliefs. In addition, the autonomous learning activity is placed temporally and situationally among other activities thereby affecting motivational considerations within the agent.

3. E $\rightarrow$ B $\rightarrow$ P $\rightarrow$ E:

The environment facilitates/impedes autonomous learning thereby changing the agent in a manner that affects those who surround the agent.

4. E $\rightarrow$ P $\rightarrow$ B $\rightarrow$ E:

The environment influences the motivation to engage in autonomous learning that involves focusing on aspects of an imposed environment or selecting/creating environments conducive to learning. In addition, this learning activity, when observed, affects others.

5. B $\rightarrow$ P $\rightarrow$ E $\rightarrow$ B:

Autonomous learning produces outcomes, efficacy information, and new knowledge or skills that create observable changes in the agent so that others choose to facilitate or impede autonomous learning.

6. B $\rightarrow$ E $\rightarrow$ P $\rightarrow$ B:

The agent selects or creates an environment conducive to learning. This learning activity, when observed, affects others and the manner in which they interact with the agent. In addition, the autonomous learning activity is placed temporally and situationally among other activities thereby affecting motivational considerations within the agent that influence future participation in autonomous learning.

Rebounding Processes

Direct and mediating effects also provide for "rebounding" processes. Three examples are as follows:

1. E $\rightarrow$ B $\rightarrow$ P $\rightarrow$ B:

The environment facilitates/impedes autonomous learning and creates outcomes that are desirable or undesirable thereby changing the agent in a manner that affects how the agent intentionally engages in autonomous learning.

2. $P \rightarrow B \rightarrow E \rightarrow B$:
The agent intentionally engages in autonomous learning by selecting or creating an environment conducive to learning. This learning activity, when observed, affects others who can facilitate or impede autonomous learning directly.

3. $E \rightarrow P \rightarrow B \rightarrow P$:
The environment presents to the person a repertoire of people from which the agent chooses and appraises a model in order to inform efficacy beliefs (i.e., vicarious experience).

The previous description of various interactions is not an attempt to offer any particular path analytic model but rather an attempt to reveal the rich complexity of implications associated with the TRC model that has no "beginning" or "ending" point; human action can be catalyzed in a multitude of ways that vary in time due to personological, environmental, or behavioral dynamics. It is quite likely that there are additional psychosocial constructs as well as different interpretations of the interactions highlighted that can be used to continue this discussion. In addition, further discussion can consider both interdeterminant interactions (e.g., many actions covary as do "situational happenings"; Bandura, 1986, p. 25) as well as temporal dynamics (i.e., interactions may be immediate or separated greatly in time; Bandura, 1986).

To learn means to change with respect to acquiring knowledge or skills thereby influencing—in addition to being influenced by—how one thinks, feels, and acts; however, understanding the phenomenon of learning cannot be understood outside of context. That is, when there is agency in learning (i.e., intentional learning under the learner's control), there must be a consideration of the following questions: (a) why learn? (b) what to learn? (c) when to learn? (d) how much to learn? (e) how long to learn? and (f) how to learn? All of these questions are answered by an agent who already has developed in a unique manner based upon previous learning.

But previous learning is dependent upon interactions between the agent and the environment as well as his or her behaviors; the focus of analysis is not merely on the agent. We learn from others either by direct instruction or by observation, we learn from ourselves as we make sense of our actions, and the manner and degree that we are able to learn from others or ourselves is influenced by how much we have already learned from others or ourselves. Personal development—learning—cannot be understood by focusing solely on the person despite the fact that this is where learning occurs (i.e., no one can learn for someone else).

Similarly, the answers to the aforementioned questions cannot be understood by a singular personological focus. A simple conclusion of motivation theory is that at any given instant we do what we are most motivated to do; however, life is a series of instants in which there is great variation in the things we do resulting from the vacillations of our motivation. As we age, we have a relatively stable value system resulting from our previous learning, but we also have temporally unstable situational factors that interact with our value system thereby influencing our motivation to act at any given moment. The varied answers to these questions—particularly the first five—are a result of this dynamic interplay.

The sixth question—how to learn—introduces the varied modes of agency through which our personal agency can be exercised. When we are motivated to learn, we can allow others to create our learning activity (i.e., proxy agency), work with others to create a learning activity (i.e., collective agency), or create a learning activity all on our own (i.e., individual agency); however, regardless of the mode, all three are catalyzed by our personal agency to intentionally learn something of personal value. The particular mode that is chosen, though, is based upon a consideration of not only utility (i.e., how well the mode may help us learn) but also self-efficacy; that is, we must believe that we are capable of enacting the mode to create an effective learning activity. As already discussed, the strengthening of efficacy appraisals is rooted in the interplay of person, environment, and behavior.

Concluding Remarks

This chapter represents an attempt to offer a more complete discussion of the vast complexity associated with the phenomenon of agency in general and autonomous learning in particular as suggested by the TRC model (cf. Ponton & Rhea, 2006). A conclusion, however, should not be that to understand autonomous learning one must understand every conceivable construct and every conceivable interaction. There are likely a limited set of constructs and interactions that offer the greatest predictive power and explanatory utility to both understanding and, ultimately, facilitating autonomous learning, and specific environments (e.g., a given educational or corporate setting) may offer controls for certain constructs and interactions that promote parsimonious models with limited application. For all theory building, however, interactions associated with the TRC model's three determinants should be considered to as great an extent as is reasonable in order to capture the rich complexity of human agency.

References

Atkinson, J. W. (1964). *An introduction to motivation*. Princeton, NJ: D. Van Nostrand.

Bandura, A. (1986). *Social foundations of thought and action: A social cognitive theory*. Englewood Cliffs, NJ: Prentice Hall.

Bandura, A. (1989). Human agency in social cognitive theory. *American Psychologist, 44*(9), 1175-1184.

Bandura, A. (1997). *Self-efficacy: The exercise of control*. New York, NY: W. H. Freeman and Company.

Bandura, A. (2006). Toward a psychology of human agency. *Perspectives on Psychological Science, 1*(2), 164-180.

Bussey, K., & Bandura, A. (1999). Social cognitive theory of gender development and differentiation. *Psychological Review, 106*(4), 676-713.

Carr, P. B. (1999). *The measurement of resourcefulness intentions in the adult autonomous learner* (Unpublished doctoral dissertation). The George Washington University, Washington, DC.

Confessore, G. J. (1991). Human behavior as a construct for assessing Guglielmino's Self-Directed Learning Readiness Scale: Pragmatism revisited. In H. B. Long & Associates (Eds.), *Self-directed learning: Consensus & conflict* (pp. 123-146). Norman, OK: Oklahoma Research Center for Continuing Professional and Higher Education of the University of Oklahoma.

Derrick, M. G. (2001). *The measurement of an adult's intention to exhibit persistence in autonomous learning* (Unpublished doctoral dissertation). The George Washington University, Washington, DC.

Fishbein, M., & Ajzen, I. (1975). *Belief, attitude, intention, and behavior: An introduction to theory and research*. Reading, MA: Addison-Wesley.

Locke, E. A., & Latham, G. P. (1990). *A theory of goal setting & task performance*. Englewood Cliffs, NJ: Prentice Hall.

Meyer, D. T. (2001). *The measurement of intentional behavior as a prerequisite to autonomous learning* (Unpublished doctoral dissertation). The George Washington University, Washington, DC.

Ponton, M. K. (1999). *The measurement of an adult's intention to exhibit personal initiative in autonomous learning* (Unpublished doctoral dissertation). The George Washington University, Washington, DC.

Ponton, M. K. (2009). An agentic perspective contrasting autonomous learning with self-directed learning. In M. G. Derrick & M. K. Ponton (Eds.), *Emerging directions in self-directed learning* (pp. 65-76). Chicago, IL: Discovery Association Publishing House. **[cf. Chapter 4]**

Ponton, M. K., & Carr, P. B. (1999). *A quasi-linear behavioral model and an application to self-directed learning* (NASA Technical Memorandum 209094). Hampton, VA: NASA Langley Research Center. **[cf. Chapter 1]**

Ponton, M. K., & Carr, P. B. (2000). Understanding and promoting autonomy in self-directed learning. *Current Research in Social Psychology, 5*(19). Retrieved from http://www.uiowa.edu/crisp/ **[cf. Chapter 2]**

Ponton, M. K., Derrick, M. G., & Carr, P. B. (2005). The relationship between resourcefulness and persistence in adult autonomous learning. *Adult Education Quarterly, 55*(2), 116-128. **[cf. Chapter 9]**

Ponton, M. K., & Rhea, N. E. (2006). Autonomous learning from a social cognitive perspective. *New Horizons in Adult Education and Human Resource Development, 20*(2), 38-49. **[cf. Chapter 3]**

CHAPTER 7

IMPOSED ENVIRONMENTS: THE IMPORTANT ROLE OF FORTUITOUS INTERSECTIONS[7]

Scholars in self-directed and autonomous learning typically have adopted an agentic perspective of these phenomena that includes the characteristic of forethought; however, unanticipated fortuitous intersections with imposed aspects of the environment can catalyze such agency thereby influencing entire life trajectories. The purpose of this chapter is to discuss the role of fortuitous intersections in order to further our understanding of personal agency as manifest in learning.

Historically scholars in self-directed and autonomous learning (e.g., Bouchard, 1994; Brockett, 1985; Candy, 1990; Chene, 1983; Confessore & Confessore, 1994; Garrison, 1989; Guglielmino, 1977; Hiemstra, 1994; Jarvis, 1992; Knowles, 1975; Long, 1989; Mezirow, 1985; Redding & Aagaard, 1992) have adopted perspectives through which to interpret these phenomena that include tenets consistent with agency theory such as control and choice. In general, human agency has the following characteristics: (a) *forethought* is enlisted to prioritize desirable outcomes, establish goals, and create plans to satisfy personally realized needs; (b) subsequent action is then characterized as being *intentional*; (c) the agent *self-reacts* to cognized plans and engages in action; and (d) the agent *self-reflects* upon the consequences of the action to both extract meaning and decide upon further action (Bandura, 2006). Using this conceptual framework, the autonomous learner uses forethought to ideate learning goals and activities believed to lead to desirable outcomes; intentionally reacts to this cognition by choosing to select/create and participate in learning activities; and reflects upon the consequences of these activities thereby resulting in learning that influences future learning with respect to both the interpretation of new knowledge, skills, or attitudes as well as the design of subsequent learning activities (Ponton, 2009).

---

[7]Paper presented at the 29th International Self-Directed Learning Symposium (2015)

This perspective is seemingly devoid of the environment; that is, this description suggests a bidirectional, cognitivistic relationship between person (i.e., beliefs, attitudes, and intentions) and behavior (cf. Fishbein & Azjen, 1975). However, the environment plays a crucial role in (a) developing within the agent comparative value of possible outcomes and, thus, pursuits; (b) informing percepts of self-efficacy that influence the motivation to choose, participate, and persevere in given pursuits; (c) providing opportunities as well as limits to personal agency; and (d) facilitating intersections of information—intended or imposed—that the agent uses to decide courses of action (Bandura, 1986). In addition, the agent influences the environment by objective alteration (i.e., intentionally via purposeful change or unintentionally via how others react merely to the agent's presence) or subjective interpretation (i.e., the environment takes on meaning via the agent's perspective).

Beginning at birth, the life trajectories of people begin their unique courses. Not only is there fortuity—that is, occurrences due to chance rather than intention—in initial conditions (i.e., there was no agency on the part of the neonate to choose either the characteristics of the immediate environment or personal physical/mental state/capacities) but also in future conditions due to unintended intersections with imposed environmental aspects. Although personal agency exerts a determinative influence throughout an entire existence, personal paths are anything but deterministic (Bandura, 1982). The importance of considering fortuitous intersections rests in the notion that the lives of people, which are easily observed to vary considerably, cannot be understood by merely modeling agency as a proactive force; humans agentically react to unintended environmental happenings. Thus, agentic responses to fortuitous beginnings and happenings result in unique lives (Bandura, 1982).

Reciprocal determinism, as modeled by triadic reciprocal causation, recognizes that human functioning represents an interplay between person, environment, and behavior (Bandura, 1986). All three factors interact in personologically and situationally time-dependent ways thereby resulting in unpredictable life courses between people with one aspect of this unpredictability due to fortuitous happenings. However, a mere understanding of fortuitous intersections cannot explain human functioning in a manner that supports environmentalism. Such intersections must be recognized as factors that can influence a person's agentic response that then operates reciprocally to influence the environment, the person, and the chance of future fortuitous intersections with their own consequences. In this regard, fortuitous intersections may be understood as both proactive causes and reactive effects of human agency (cf. Bandura, 1998). The purpose of this chapter is discuss the role of imposed environments as manifest in fortuitous intersections in order to further our understanding of agency in learning.

Modes and Environmental Manifestations of Personal Agency

The exhibition of personal agency in one's chosen pursuit does not necessarily limit activity to social isolation; others may be involved to varying degrees. Hence, personal agency may be manifest through three modes: collective, proxy, or individual (Bandura, 2006). Personal agency via the collective mode occurs when an agent decides to enlist the assistance of others and works with them in determining an activity that can accomplish the agent's goal. Proxy agency occurs when the agent enlists the help of others and allows them to act independently in determining an activity that supports the agent's goal. Individual agency occurs when the agent acts alone in determining an activity. In all three modes, however, personal agency is still the catalyst for action; that is, it is the agent who engages in forethought, intentionality, self-reaction, and self-reflection with respect to the particular mode of agency invoked for his or her chosen purpose (Bandura, 2006).

Reciprocal determinism suggests that environmental aspects can be manifest in three forms: created, selected, or imposed (Bandura, 1997). Created aspects are features that did not exist until the agent created them; for example, a learner can create a learning activity that includes a goal, plan (includes the selection of resources, method for interaction with the resources, and contingencies to manage impediments), participation, assessment of learning and satisfaction, and adjustment based upon the assessment. The learning activity is environmental because an observer can witness the learner engaging in the activity; that is, there is an objective manifestation. Conversely, an agent can intentionally select aspects of his or her environment from those that already exist; for example, a learner can select from a multitude of already created learning activities such as college courses. Imposed aspects refer to environmental features that are not the result of personal agency in selection or creation; that is, features that are—with respect to the person—unintended and, thus, fortuitous. Although the intersection between the person and the environmental aspect is fortuitous, subsequent action with respect to the imposed aspect is governed by personal agency (Bandura, 2006) in that the person acting as an agent can choose how much attention to provide to this aspect and whether or not to select or create activities as a response.

Using both the mode of agency invoked as well as the environmental agentic action, Figure 1 presents a matrix of possible agentic manifestations with cell descriptions as follows:

MODE OF PERSONAL AGENCY

	Collective	Proxy	Individual
Select	1	2	3
Create	4	5	6

ENVIRONMENTAL ACTION

Figure 1. Six possible manifestations of personal agency with the environment.

Cell 1. An agent enlists the help of others and works with them to select from the environment an existing activity that the agent anticipates will lead to a personally desirable consequence.

Cell 2. An agent enlists the help of others and allows them to select from the environment an existing activity that the agent anticipates will lead to a personally desirable consequence.

Cell 3. An agent works alone to select from the environment an existing activity that the agent anticipates will lead to a personally desirable consequence.

Cell 4. An agent enlists the help of others and works with them to create a new activity that the agent anticipates will lead to a personally desirable consequence.

Cell 5. An agent enlists the help of others and allows them to create a new activity that the agent anticipates will lead to a personally desirable consequence.

95

Cell 6. An agent works alone to create a new activity that the agent anticipates will lead to a personally desirable consequence.

When the context for the activity is learning, the agent who participates in the learning activity can be described as an autonomous learner. That is, the agent is exhibiting autonomy in choosing to either select or create a learning activity with or without the help of others; after selection or creation, learning occurs through participation. Examples of the varied manifestations of autonomous learning are as follows:

Cell 1. A teenager chooses to work with his or her parents in order to select a given university and program of study.

Cell 2. After enrolling in a university's program, a student allows a faculty member to prescribe the curriculum from existing courses.

Cell 3. A person with an interest in photography selects a short course offered by a municipality.

Cell 4. A mechanical engineer with an electronics problem chooses to work with an electrical engineer in order to identify required learning topics and reference books.

Cell 5. A manager hires an educational consulting firm to conduct a needs assessment and create a custom series of training modules.

Cell 6. A person with an interest in Egyptian pyramids identifies a book, reads it, and assesses personal satisfaction with the resultant learning.

In this regard, *agentic learning* is synonymous with *autonomous learning* in that the latter is the result of personal agency as manifest in learning (Ponton & Rhea, 2006).

Self-Directed Learning

As a special case of autonomous learning, self-directed learning (SDL) refers to cell 6 (see Figure 1); that is, the self-directed learner chooses to individually create (i.e., decide upon) all aspects of the learning activity as previously described (i.e., the goal, plan, assessment, and adjustment; Ponton, 2009). Only in this regard can the learner be described as self directing the learning. This does not mean that the SDL activity must occur in social isolation; it may not if the self-directed learner identifies others as learning resources (i.e., sources of information). This classification merely recognizes that it is the self-directed learner who acts as an agent in choosing to individually create all aspects of the learning activity. If the self-directed learner chooses others as learning resources (similar to nonhuman sources of information such as books), this does not reduce the learner's total control over choosing, designing, and participating in the activity.

Following this assertion, a learner who participates in a course in which the instructor facilitates aspects of self-direction in a learning activity is not engaged in a SDL activity; that is, SDL requires the learner to choose to create the learning activity as a result of personal agency, which means that it is at the learner's discretion to do so. If an instructor requires a student to create a goal, plan, assessment, and perhaps adjustments subsequent to participation—that is, create and participate in a learning activity—the instructor is still in control of the activity because the activity is the result of the instructor's agency as a teacher rather than the student's as a learner.

Of course there can be episodes of SDL when one takes a course. A recurring situation is when a student encounters a concept of unfamiliar meaning. In response to this situation, the student can choose to individually create and participate in a learning activity—no matter how brief—with a goal (i.e., understanding), plan (e.g., use a dictionary), participation (e.g., read), assessment (i.e., satisfaction with resultant learning), and adjustment (i.e., if not satisfied, develop a new plan; e.g., conduct an Internet search). In this situation, the student has invoked personal agency to engage in self-directed learning and has chosen to exert complete control over creating and participating in a learning activity in which he or she directs all aspects.

This description of SDL suggests that it is categorical; that is, SDL does not exist on a continuum. When direction—no matter how slight—is provided by another, then the activity is no longer SDL; the activity is still an autonomous learning activity provided it is the result of the learner's personal agency. On the contrary, self-directedness—a person's predisposition to engage in SDL—does fall on a continuum (Brockett, 1994) as the propensity to engage in SDL varies personologically (i.e., dependent upon the person's characteristics) and situationally (i.e., dependent upon the topic, urgency, and available means). Similarly, autonomous learning is categorical, and learner autonomy is continuous.

The present description of SDL does not presume that it is essentially "better" than other types of autonomous learning activities in any overall sense. This description is merely a classification of a particular learning phenomenon. Optimal learning can and often does occur when others with more knowledge or skill are purposefully given control over directing aspects of the learning activity; "everyday functioning requires an agentic blend" (Bandura, 2006, p. 165). There is also value in learning that occurs nonagentically. However, a high level of self-directedness does offer one important benefit: in the absence of others who could provide direction, learning—at least to some degree—can still occur. Thus, a high level of self-directedness enables a person to continually develop along intentional trajectories when others are not available to provide any direction no matter how slight.

Types of Fortuitous Intersections

Imposed environmental aspects create fortuitous (i.e., unintended) intersections between a person and the environment. For example, a person might encounter a stranger at a coffee shop that leads to conversing, dating, marrying, and redirecting an entire life's trajectory from a direction that would not have occurred if the person had forgone or even slightly delayed the coffee shop visit. In this example, the only initial agency invoked was the decision and subsequent action of acquiring coffee at a given place and time. Although the fortuitous intersection was not caused by an autonomous learning event, subsequent agency in learning was exerted in choosing to learn about this unanticipated person via intentional conversation and dating.

Agency plays an important role in increasing the opportunities for fortuitous intersections to occur. An agent who intentionally engages with the environment through varied activities creates opportunities for unanticipated occurrences; in contrast, the person who sits at home, does nothing, and waits for opportunity to knock creates little opportunity to fortuitously intersect with new topics, people, or other environmental aspects. As in the previous example, fortuity as manifest in imposed environmental aspects can be the result of personal agency in nonlearning activities; however, once experienced, the agent can then react to these happenings by agentically choosing to learn (see Figure 2, cell 1).

Fortuity can also characterize imposed happenings unrelated to any agency. An example would be becoming ill due to a genetic predisposition. The corresponding imposed environment would include the initial physician's visit, diagnosis, subsequent visits, treatments, or lifestyle changes. Despite no initial agency in causing the fortuitous intersection, the response to such fortuity may be an agentic decision to engage in learning in order to cope with the malady (see Figure 2, cell 3).

Cells 1 and 3 (see Figure 2) describe situations that occur *before* the agent decides to engage in a learning activity with such events influencing subsequent decisions to engage in autonomous learning. Such events are often referred to as "triggering" events as they can trigger or catalyze learning. In contrast, fortuitous intersections can also occur *after* an agent decides to engage in learning (cells 2 and 4 in Figure 2).

<table>
<tr><td></td><td></td><td colspan="2" align="center">TEMPORAL RELATION TO
LEARNING DECISION</td></tr>
<tr><td></td><td></td><td align="center">Before</td><td align="center">After</td></tr>
<tr><td rowspan="2">CAUSE OF
OPPORTUNITY
FOR THE
IMPOSED
ENVIRONMENTAL
ASPECT</td><td>Agentic</td><td align="center">1</td><td align="center">2</td></tr>
<tr><td>Nonagentic</td><td align="center">3</td><td align="center">4</td></tr>
</table>

Figure 2. Temporal and agentic possibilities between imposed environments and learning decisions.

After a person decides to learn about a topic, he or she can canvass the learning resources that happen to be available (see Figure 2, cell 4); that is, resources that were not selected from the universe of possible resources but rather are fortuitously present (Spear & Mocker, 1984). Before the ubiquity of Internet-based technologies, the primary household source of information was the paper based encyclopedia, which was a resource of a seemingly unknown origin as its age could far exceed that of the household's inhabitants. This compendium of information on various topics represented a convenient resource often used exclusively to address myriad questions of personal interest to the great extent that if a question could not be answered via the encyclopedia, it remained unanswered. Hence, the cause of the opportunity for the imposed environmental aspect—the encyclopedia—

was not due to the agency of the learner. Despite that such a resource is fortuitously present (i.e., not intentionally selected and made available for a particular learning event by the agent but was present by chance), the chance of intersecting with the resource was high due to convenience and lack of alternatives.

Imposed environmental aspects also include topics or people unrelated to the intended purpose of an autonomous learning activity (see Figure 2, cell 2). In the previous encyclopedic example, once accessed—that is, once personal agency in learning was invoked—the encyclopedia could support a series of searches with subsequent learning events catalyzed by a fortuitous intersection with a topic in a previous search. As a more current example, accessing Internet-based media in pursuit of specific information often leads to fortuitous intersections with topics unrelated to the initial inquiry that spawn inquiry in new directions; in fact, Webpages are often designed to facilitate this dynamic process by not only providing such unrelated topics but also by making associated information easily accessible via embedded hyperlinks. The encyclopedic example is analogous to the Internet-based example; however, the latter has reduced limitations in content (i.e., there is seemingly an endless supply of topics and information in a variety of forms) and access (i.e., smart phones and tablets are easily carried) while increasing the presence of unrelated topics (e.g., a search for one news topic typically leads to Webpages filled with unrelated news topics). An example of fortuitous intersections with both topics and people is when a learner decides to take a course from an institution in order to satisfy a personal interest. By giving control to the instructor in selecting learning resources and to the institution in admitting students and hiring faculty, the learner can fortuitously intersect (and likely does) with unanticipated topics *and* people that can greatly influence future learning and, thus, personal trajectories. In these examples, the cause of the opportunity for the imposed environmental aspect—the new topic or person—was due to the agency of the learner to engage in an autonomous learning activity. Once the fortuitous intersection occurs, it is the learner who then continues to exert personal agency in choosing whether or not, to what degree, and how new learning will occur. This imposed environment becomes part of an environmental potentiality from which the agent creates a personal environment.

The Continuum of Chance

A typical characteristic of learning is that there will be new (i.e., unknown) topics encountered. When the learning is autonomous (i.e., when the learning activity is chosen by the agent for an intended purpose manifest in the pursuit of a given topic) such new topics can be (a) objectively-related to the desired topic, (b) subjectively-related, or (c) unrelated. Examples are as follows:

- Objectively-related. A study of the life of Abraham Lincoln includes some study of the U.S. Civil War.
- Subjectively-related. A study of higher education administration includes some study of self-directed learning.
- Unrelated. A study of surfboarding includes some study of Abraham Lincoln.

In this regard, the degree of chance in intersecting with a new topic exists on a continuum due to the "subjectively-related" category; that is, human arguments regarding relatedness can be highly subjective thereby causing included topics to be unpredictable. This can be manifest via seemingly identical learning resources. As examples, the topics covered in similarly titled courses can vary by faculty while those in similarly titled books can vary author; in each case, the arguments of topic relatedness to the title are made by the creator of the learning opportunity. Note, too, that not only is topic relatedness subject to argument but also the extent (with, perhaps, additional topics) to which subjectively-related topics are covered. Exact probabilities of chance based upon subjective arguments are incapable of calculation; thus, the purpose of this perspective is merely to undergird a conceptual model (see Figure 3).

As mentioned, fortuitous intersections with people are also possible during autonomous learning activities. Several examples of opportunities for such intersections are as follows: when selecting a college course section based solely upon schedule, no consideration is given regarding the instructor or other enrollees; in a face-to-face class, seating positions can occur based primarily upon availability; in an online course, students from around the world are able to enroll in the same course. Due to these uncontrolled and, thus, unpredictable arrangements of people with potentially varied backgrounds, resultant intersections between people are fortuitous, and associated conversations represent fortuitous intersections with topics that relate to varying degrees with the intended topic.

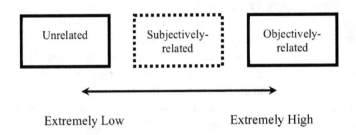

Figure 3. The degree of chance of fortuitous intersections with topics and people: a continuum based upon relatedness to the initial topic.

In the extreme, relationships are often formed based upon backgrounds and conversations entirely unrelated to the learning activity that brought the people together; in this situation, the fortuitous intersection between the people is characterized as unrelated to the initial topic. For example, there is an extremely low chance that an instructor and a student (who is 20 years younger) participating in a higher education administration program will discuss their fathers' army service that occurred at the same place and time 40 years earlier (which, in fact, did occur). In the objectively-related situation, backgrounds and conversations are aligned with the intended topic; for example, there is an extremely high chance that a mathematics instructor will discuss differentiation with mathematics majors in a calculus course. In the subjectively-related situation, backgrounds and conversations are arguably related to the intended topic; for example, an American history major electively enrolls in an economics course and converses with an engineering major about the Great Depression. Similar to the previous discussion regarding topics, the degree of subjective relatedness to the initial topic is based upon human arguments; therefore, the degree of chance for fortuitous intersections with people is also represented by a continuum (see Figure 3).

Facilitating Fortuitous Intersections via Autonomous Learning

The greater a person pursues learning in various ways and on various topics, the greater the likelihood that he or she will intersect with unanticipated topics or people in the environment. Thus, autonomous learning influences pathways to diverse information upon which the learner can exert personal agency in shaping his or her life in unique ways. An increase of fortuitous intersections increases the choices agents have in directing their respective lives. Thus, strengthening learner autonomy is an essential factor in expanding life's possibilities.

When an autonomous learner chooses to engage in a course, the instructor can play an important role in facilitating fortuitous intersections. By creating a topic rich environment (i.e., an inclusion of many topics subjectively related to the course's focus) and assignments to pursue self-selected interests, the instructor provides not only the seed for divergent growth between students but also the opportunity for individually chosen growth among students. The concomitant control and resultant personal satisfaction in such self-selected pursuits strengthens learner autonomy by building efficacy and motivation thereby resulting in students becoming agents of their own development. By strengthening students' learner autonomy, they are able to increase the likelihood of more fortuitous intersections in other self-selected learning endeavors.

Instructors can also facilitate fortuitous intersections between people. Although discussion as well as team and group activities are typically used to support instruction, resultant interactions provide opportunities for students to converse with others—students or faculty—on matters that have varying degrees of relatedness to the course's topic. Such interactions can spawn relationships that transcend the course in both topic and time.

Concluding Remarks

Extant conceptions of human agency adopt a goal-directed perspective: the agent selects a goal, decides how to reach this goal, acts toward reaching this goal, evaluates progress, and corrects action if deemed necessary. When the goal is a learning goal, the agent engages in (some form of) autonomous learning. The existence of fortuitous intersections with topics, people, or other environmental happenings is not antithetical to this agentic description.

However, fortuitous intersections must be considered in order to understand the variability between the specific goals adopted by different people thereby resulting in different lives. In this regard, fortuitous intersections with imposed environments offer branching points in a life's trajectory. Such intersections provide information that is individually considered when choosing the next goal to pursue. Thus, agency is invoked as a response to such chance environmental happenings. Agentic responses then create opportunities for new fortuitous intersections to occur with their own possibilities as branching points. Hence, fortuitous intersections manifest as both causes and effects of human agency.

In order to understand the lived experience, one must not only understand the important determining role that human agency plays but also the information upon which such agency is invoked. In this regard, agentic determinism does not mean that lives are deterministic due, in large part, to unintended, fortuitous intersections with environmental impositions. Self-reflection of one's personal narrative will likely provide supporting evidence for this assertion.

References

Bandura, A. (1982). The psychology of chance encounters and life paths. *American Psychologist, 37*(7), 747-755.

Bandura, A. (1986). *Social foundations of thought and action: A social cognitive theory.* Englewood Cliffs, NJ: Prentice Hall.

Bandura, A. (1997). *Self-efficacy: The exercise of control.* New York, NY: W. H. Freeman and Company.

Bandura, A. (1998). Exploration of fortuitous determinants of life paths. *Psychological Inquiry, 9*(2), 95-115.

Bandura, A. (2006). Toward a psychology of human agency. *Perspectives on Psychological Science, 1*(2), 164-180.

Bouchard, P. (1994). Self-directed professionals and autodidactic choice. In H. B. Long & Associates (Eds.), *New ideas about self-directed learning* (pp. 121-137). Norman, OK: Oklahoma Research Center for Continuing Professional and Higher Education of the University of Oklahoma.

Brockett, R. G. (1985). The relationship between self-directed learning readiness and life satisfaction among older adults. *Adult Education Quarterly, 35*(4), 210-219.

Brockett, R. G. (1994). Resistance to self-direction in adult learning: Myths and misunderstandings. In R. Hiemstra & R. G. Brockett (Eds.), *Overcoming resistance in self-direction in adult learning* (pp. 5-12). San Francisco, CA: Jossey-Bass.

Candy, P. D. (1990). The transition from learner-control to autodidaxy: More than meets the eye. In H. B. Long & Associates (Eds.), *Advances in research and practice in self-directed learning* (pp. 9-46). Norman, OK: Oklahoma Research Center for Continuing Professional and Higher Education of the University of Oklahoma.

Chene, A. (1983). The concept of autonomy in adult education: A philosophical discussion. *Adult Education Quarterly, 34*(1), 38-47.

Confessore, S. J., & Confessore, G. J. (1994). Learner profiles: A cross-sectional study of selected factors associated with self-directed learning. In H. B. Long & Associates (Eds.), *New ideas about self-directed learning* (pp. 201-227). Norman, OK: Oklahoma Research Center for Continuing Professional and Higher Education of the University of Oklahoma.

Fishbein, M., & Ajzen, I. (1975). *Belief, attitude, intention, and behavior: An introduction to theory and research.* Reading, MA: Addison-Wesley.

Garrison, D. R. (1989). Facilitating self-directed learning: Not a contradiction in terms. In H. B. Long & Associates (Eds.), *Self-directed learning: Emerging theory & practice* (pp. 53-62). Norman, OK: Oklahoma Research Center for Continuing Professional and Higher Education of the University of Oklahoma.

Guglielmino, L. M. (1977). *Development of the self-directed learning readiness scale* (Doctoral dissertation). Retrieved from ProQuest Dissertations & Theses Global. (Accession No. 7806004)

Hiemstra, R. (1994). Self-directed learning. In T. Husen & T. N. Postlethwaite (Eds.), *The international encyclopedia of education* (2nd ed.). Oxford, UK: Pergamon Press.

Jarvis, P. (1992). Free-will, freedom and self-directed learning. In H. B. Long & Associates (Eds.), *Self-directed learning: Application and research* (pp. 97-117). Norman, OK: Oklahoma Research Center for Continuing Professional and Higher Education of the University of Oklahoma.

Knowles, M. S. (1975). *Self-directed learning: A guide for learners and teachers.* Chicago, IL: Follett.

Long, H. B. (1989). Self-directed learning: Emerging theory and practice. In H. B. Long & Associates (Eds.), *Self-directed learning: Emerging theory & practice* (pp. 1-11). Norman, OK: Oklahoma Research Center for Continuing Professional and Higher Education of the University of Oklahoma.

Mezirow, J. (1985). Concept and action in adult education. *Adult Education Quarterly, 35*(3), 142-151.

Ponton, M. K. (2009). An agentic perspective contrasting autonomous learning with self-directed learning. In M. G. Derrick & M. K. Ponton (Eds.), *Emerging directions in self-directed learning* (pp. 65-76). Chicago, IL: Discovery Association Publishing House. **[cf. Chapter 4]**

Ponton, M. K., & Rhea, N. E. (2006). Autonomous learning from a social cognitive perspective. *New Horizons in Adult Education and Human Resource Development, 20*(2), 38-49. **[cf. Chapter 3]**

Redding, T. R., & Aagaard, L. (1992). A descriptive investigation of the construct of self-direction. In H. B. Long & Associates (Eds.), *Self-directed learning: Application and research* (pp. 147-161). Norman, OK: Oklahoma Research Center for Continuing Professional and Higher Education of the University of Oklahoma.

Spear, G. E., & Mocker, D. W. (1984). The organizing circumstance: Environmental determinants in self-directed learning. *Adult Education Quarterly, 35*(1), 1-10.

CHAPTER 8

A PATH ANALYSIS OF THE CONATIVE FACTORS ASSOCIATED WITH AUTONOMOUS LEARNING[8]

It has been previously argued that autonomous learning can be defined as the presence of the following conative factors: resourcefulness, initiative, and persistence. These factors are conative in that they are predicated upon the presence of motivation to engage in autonomous learning activities. The purpose of this chapter is to present the results of a path analysis performed on these factors in an attempt to gain support of a hypothesized causal model. Because of the causal inferences presented, a better understanding of the relationship between salient aspects of autonomous learning will be suggested. The importance of this understanding is the ultimate enablement of learning facilitators to develop autonomy within learners.

The data analyzed in this chapter are from a sample of 909 adults. The demographics of the sample are as follows: 601 females and 308 males; 285 with only a high school diploma, 265 a baccalaureate degree only, and 359 with a graduate/professional degree; the age of the subjects range from 17 to 88 (M = 33.45, SD = 10.23). The data were gathered using the Learner Autonomy Profile that measures desire in a generalized context and resourcefulness, initiative, and persistence within the context of adult autonomous learning. The chapter will conclude with a recommendation that future research be performed on motivation and self-efficacy contextualized to autonomous learning activities.

Derrick (2002) asserted, "understanding the behaviors associated with persistence in learning is critical to understanding . . . why some individuals are successful and others are not successful in their learning endeavors" (p. 16). However, the premise of this chapter is that understanding perseverant behaviors is necessary but not sufficient in

---

[8]This article is reprinted with permission from the *International Journal for Self-Directed Learning* (http://sdlglobal.com/journals.php) and is copyrighted © The International Society for Self-Directed Learning [2004, *1*(1), 59-69]

fostering learning persistence within adults. What is needed is a better understanding of the causal relationships between persistence and other autonomous learning constructs (i.e., desire, resourcefulness, and persistence) to not only better prepare facilitators of learner autonomy but also to serve as a stimulus for future research. Persistence is studied as a desired result because it is posited to be the defining characteristic of learning that continues until a personally satisfying end is reached.

Theoretical Framework

Over the past 5 years, several researchers have attempted to build upon the premise of Confessore (1992) that "self-directed learning, as with any other human endeavor, becomes a matter of drive, initiative, resourcefulness, and persistence [in order for learners] to see . . . [themselves] through to some level of learning that is personally satisfying" (p. 3). These researchers have developed instrumentation that focuses on the assessment of an adult autonomous learner's desire (cf. Meyer, 2001), resourcefulness (Carr, 1999), initiative (Ponton, 1999), and persistence (Derrick, 2001) with continual testing to help make tenable each instrument's validity and reliability (cf. Ponton & Carr, 2002).

In a general sense, Meyer (2001) created an instrument that assesses an adult's ability to exert influence over his or her life based upon three constituent processes: freedom, power, and change. Therefore, while Meyer's instrument does not measure desire within the context of adult autonomous learning, her instrument attempts to measure the degree to which an agent can act intentionally. The connection to desire (i.e., from a motivational perspective) exists through the process of self-efficacy, a construct that has been shown to mediate all theories of cognitive motivation (Bandura, 1997). As Park and Confessore (2002) asserted, "[Meyer's] work on desire to learn has been treated as an effort to understand the *precursors* to the development of intentions related to learning" (p. 289).

The premise of Carr's (1999) work is that resourcefulness represents a syndrome of behavioral self-control skills that transcend the dichotomy of redressive and reformative self-control (cf. Rosenbaum, 1989) thereby resulting in the following four behaviors indicative of autonomous learning: (a) prioritizing learning activities over nonlearning activities; (b) choosing to engage in learning activities as opposed to nonlearning activities; (c) looking to the future benefits of present learning; and (d) solving problems that interfere with learning activities. Problem solving includes the ability to plan learning activities, evaluate different learning activities, and anticipate the consequences of different activities. The term *resourcefulness* is used because it represents the collection of skills that a learner uses to cope with the stress associated with learning. Carr developed instrumentation that assesses an adult's intention to show resourcefulness in autonomous learning activities.

Building upon the work of other research on personal initiative (primarily from the field of business), Ponton (1999) created an instrument that measures five behavioral intentions in an adult autonomous learner: (a) goal-directedness; (b) action-orientation; (c) persistence in overcoming obstacles; (d) active-approach to problem solving; and (e) self-startedness. Goal-directedness refers to the creation of learning goals and working toward their accomplishment, action-orientation refers to quickly moving from an intention to learn to actual learning, persistence in overcoming obstacles refers to continued pursuit of learning in spite of the presence of impediments, active-approach to problem solving is indicative of a learner that develops solution strategies to deal with impediments without waiting on someone else to develop such strategies, and self-startedness refers to being able to self-start learning activities and their associated processes (e.g., goal setting and planning).

Derrick (2002) conceptualized persistence as the sustained maintenance of three behaviors: volition, self-regulation, and goal-directedness. Volition represents the motivation to sustain an intended behavior while self-regulation refers to maintaining activities that coincide with one's integrated self (accomplished primarily through self-reflective judgment). Although Ponton (1999) included goal-directedness as a behavior of personal initiative, Derrick provided the added criterion of perseverance toward goal accomplishment to differentiate this subscale from his.

Research Problem

While much of the previous research has focused on establishing the validity and reliability of the four instruments, little work has been published that addresses the linear relationship between the four constructs of desire, resourcefulness, initiative, and persistence. Of deeper importance, no causal modeling has been performed that may suggest a relationship between these four constructs. Such work is necessary to further our understanding of autonomous learning and suggest avenues for future research.

Research Purpose

Ponton and Carr (2000) attempted to highlight common critical facets associated with the three conative factors of resourcefulness, initiative, and persistence in an attempt to better enable an educator to foster autonomy within students. However, their discussion was general in nature without regard to the potential influence of cause and effect relationships. The purpose of this research is to theorize a causal model for desire, resourcefulness, initiative, and persistence and then perform a path analysis to determine the tenability of the hypothesized model.

Methodology

The four respective instruments of Meyer, Carr, Ponton, and Derrick constitute the Learner Autonomy Profile (LAP). Each of the four instruments have been argued as being construct and content valid as well as externally and internally reliable (Park & Confessore, 2002).

The data from research performed on 909 adults are presented. These adults participated in a large cross-sectional research effort directed by Gary J. Confessore (The George Washington University) on North American, Western European, and East Asian adults from which the presented results are derived. The demographics of the sample are as follows: 601 females and 308 males; 285 with only a high school diploma, 265 a baccalaureate degree only, and 359 with a graduate/professional degree; the age of the subjects range from 17 to 88 ($M = 33.45$, $SD = 10.23$). Although a large subsample of the data represent East Asian students studying in the United States ($n = 417$) and the means of these students on all four scales are statistically lower than the remainder of the sample, trends in the linear analysis techniques (i.e., correlation and regression analyses) produced similar results; therefore, all data were used in the analysis. Data analysis was performed using the *Statistical Package for Social Sciences*.

Proposed Causal Model

As indicated in Table 1, a statistically significant ($p < .001$) linear relationship exists for all bivariate correlations of the four LAP scales. Using qualitative descriptors of Hinkle, Wiersma, and Jurs (1998, p.

120), the Pearson product-moment correlations between resourcefulness, initiative, and persistence are high while desire is only moderately correlated with resourcefulness, initiative, and persistence.

Table 1. Intercorrelations between Scales ($N = 909$)

Scale	1	2	3	4
1. Desire	—	.654**	.625**	.631**
2. Resourcefulness		—	.871**	.871**
3. Initiative			—	.880**
4. Persistence				—

**$p < .001$.

Building upon past work (Atkinson, 1964, 1982; Bandura, 1997; Bandura & Cervone, 1983; Locke & Latham, 1990; Vroom, 1964; Weiner, 1985), Ponton, Edmister, Ukeiley, and Seiner (2001) presented a discussion of cognitive motivation and the mediating role of self-efficacy. Expectancy value theory suggests that people will be motivated to engage in activities that will lead to valued outcomes or avoid aversive ones. Such outcomes may be personal (e.g., physical pleasure or pain), social (e.g., acceptance, money, ostracism), or self-evaluative (i.e., coincidence with self-standards of behavior). However, outcomes are not directly attained by the agent; performance goals are. Thus, goals are created due to the perceived correlation between goal attainment and expected outcomes. Goal theory describes the mechanism of goal establishment in fostering motivation. Self-efficacy, or one's self-perception of capability to successfully execute an activity, serves a mediating role in both expectancy value theory and goal theory as people do not, in general, choose to engage in activities that they perceive as futile endeavors.

Ponton and Carr (1999) theorized a model of learner self-directedness and self-directed learning. In their model, they suggested that self-directedness is a cognitive and affective process that leads to the conative process of self-directed learning (i.e., intentional behavior). Self-directedness is predicated upon a person's belief that self-directed learning will lead to valued outcomes (value expectancy) thereby precipitating the creation of a goal to engage in a self-directed learning activity (goal theory). Ponton and Carr further recognized the importance of self-efficacy beliefs within the context of self-directed learning; that is, before a person creates the goal of engaging in self-directed learning, an assessment is performed by the individual with respect to whether self-directed learning capability is present. Ponton (1999) later argued that learner autonomy and autonomous learning are subsets of the actions—hence, a less restrictive classification—associated with self-directedness and self-directed learning, respectively, thereby suggesting the primacy of similar motivational processes.

Resourcefulness, initiative, and persistence are referred to as conative factors because they represent intentional behaviors based upon the presence of motivation and self-efficacy. Therefore, in a causal model, resourcefulness, initiative, and persistence should follow desire (i.e., motivation).

Conceptually, resourcefulness is more closely related to expectancy value theory because the anticipation of future rewards may influence a person to prioritize learning over nonlearning activities and, thus, choose learning over nonlearning activities. However, one should keep in mind that resourcefulness as measured is still conative in that it refers to what a learner *intends to do* and not merely what a learner knows or feels. Similarly, initiative is more closely related to goal theory because of its goal-directedness subscale but still conative because it assesses the intention of a learner to create goals and work toward their accomplishment. Because motivation associated with value expectancies is a precursor to the establishment of performance goals, it is hypothesized that resourcefulness should mediate the effect of desire on persistence and should precede initiative because of the aforementioned motivational argument.

Based upon these arguments, it is hypothesized that the largest effect on persistence will be through the path

Desire → Resourcefulness → Initiative → Persistence.

In addition, desire should have a minimal direct effect on persistence when compared to the total indirect effect.

Findings

Ordinary linear regression was used to determine the path coefficients due to their correspondence to standardized regressive coefficients

(Maxim, 1999). The following regression equations were solved based upon the hypothesized causal model:

$$z_{\hat{P}} = \beta_1 z_D + \beta_2 z_R + \beta_3 z_I ,$$
$$z_{\hat{I}} = \beta_4 z_D + \beta_5 z_R ,$$
$$z_{\hat{R}} = \beta_6 z_D .$$

Note that D, R, I, and P correspond to desire, resourcefulness, initiative, and persistence, respectively. Figure 1 presents the resulting path-analytic model.

This model offers four paths from desire to persistence: one direct effect (i.e., desire to persistence) and three indirect effects (desire through initiative to persistence; desire through resourcefulness to persistence; and desire through resourcefulness and initiative to persistence). Table 2 presents the effect sizes for each of these paths.

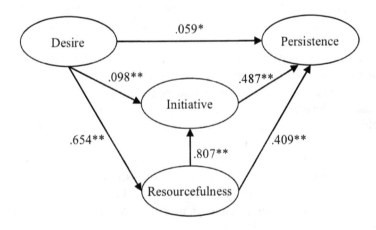

Figure 1. Overall path-analytic model: Influence of desire, initiative, and resourcefulness on persistence.
*$p = .002$; **$p < .001$.

114 |

Table 2. Effect Sizes for Different Paths

Path	Effect Size
$D \rightarrow P$	.059
$D \rightarrow I \rightarrow P$	(.098)(.487) = .048
$D \rightarrow R \rightarrow P$	(.654)(.409) = .267
$D \rightarrow R \rightarrow I \rightarrow P$	(.654)(.807)(.487) = .257

Note. The total indirect effect is .048 + .267 + .257 = .572.

As was hypothesized, the direct effect of desire on persistence is small in comparison to the total indirect effect (.059 vs. .572, respectively). In addition, the importance of the mediating role of resourcefulness, again as hypothesized, is evident in the small indirect effect of desire through initiative to persistence (.048). However, an unexpected result is the comparable indirect effects of desire through resourcefulness to persistence (.267) and desire through resourcefulness and initiative to persistence (.257). These results suggest that fostering resourcefulness in learners is a key component in facilitating persistent autonomous learning. Once resourcefulness is fostered by the learning facilitator, then personal initiative should be the educative focus.

Because desire has a small direct effect on persistence, a hierarchical regression analysis was performed to determine its predictive effect on persistence (see Table 3). Because of the important mediating role of resourcefulness, it was chosen as the baseline model (i.e., Step 1); the addition of initiative followed due to its mediating contribution (Step 2); and finally desire was added (Step 3).

While statistically significant changes in R^2 are realized with models that add initiative (Step 2) and desire (Step 3) to resourcefulness (Step 1), the practical significance of the increase associated with Step 3 is nonexistent. That is, Step 2 created an increase of 7.9% in R^2 (.759   .819) while Step 3 created an increase of only 0.2% (.819   .821). Thus, the measurement of desire, as conceptualized by Meyer (2001), has very little predictive power with respect to persistence. This is probably due to it being a general measure and not contextualized to the domain of autonomous learning. (Note that if Step 2 were the addition of desire, rather than initiative, the increase in R^2 would still be less than 1%.) Of course, the result associated with Step 3 follows the small direct effect associated with desire on persistence (note the correspondence between the Beta weights in Step 3 and the path coefficients leading to persistence in Figure 1); however, the hierarchical regression analysis provides a quantitative argument that the addition of the desire measure does not add to the prediction of persistence in any practical manner.

A second path-analytic model was computed using only the conative factors of resourcefulness, initiative, and persistence (see Figure 2). As is easily computed from the path coefficients, the direct effect of resourcefulness on persistence (.435) is comparable to the indirect effect of resourcefulness through initiative to persistence (.871 x .500 = .436).

Table 3. Summary of Hierarchical Regression Analysis for Variables Predicting Persistence ($N = 909$)

Variable	B	SE B	β
Step 1			
Resourcefulness	.603	.011	.871**
Step 2			
Resourcefulness	.301	.020	.435**
Initiative	.401	.023	.500**
Step 3			
Resourcefulness	.283	.021	.409**
Initiative	.390	.023	.487**
Desire	.067	.021	.059*

Note. $R^2 = .759$ for Step 1; $\Delta R^2 = .060$ for Step 2 ($p < .001$ for change); $\Delta R^2 = .002$ for Step 3 ($p = .002$ for change).
*$p = .002$; **$p < .001$.

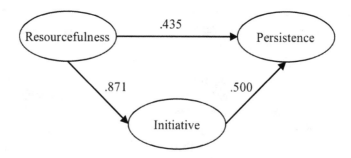

Figure 2. Reduced path-analytic model: Influence of initiative and resourcefulness on persistence. All path coefficients are significant at the 0.001 level.

Discussion

The important role of resourcefulness on persistence should not be surprising. While Carr (1999) has argued convincingly that his instrument was designed to measure *intention*, resourcefulness intention may be highly correlated with cognitive motivation. For example, an intention to choose learning activities over nonlearning activities (i.e., a conative process) may suggest greater value expectancy with learning as opposed to nonlearning (i.e., a cognitive process). However, this assertion must be tested. Cognition and affection are conceptually separable from conation and intentional behaviors; thus, instrument phraseology that attempts to assess cognitive motivation must be designed accordingly. What is of paramount importance, though, is that such motivation instrumentation is contextualized to autonomous learning similar to Carr's instrument. It should be obvious that one's motivation to engage in autonomous learning may be quite different from one's motivation to paint a house.

Similar arguments may be made for self-efficacy measures. Bandura (1995) argued that beliefs in self-efficacy have an inverse relationship to anxiety. As has already been stated, resourcefulness is related to a learner's ability to autonomously manage the stress associated with learning; thus, higher levels of resourcefulness should be positively correlated with self-efficacy. But again, this hypothesis must be tested as Carr's instrument does not measure self-efficacy. Similar to measures of motivation, self-efficacy measures must also be contextualized to the domain of autonomous learning; one's perceived ability to show resourcefulness, initiative, and persistence in learning (a.k.a., autonomous learning) may be quite different than one's perceived ability to build a nuclear reactor.

From the path model, the relationship of initiative to persistence may be explained by the relationship between expectancy value theory and goal theory. As has already been posited, the development of specific performance goals follows value expectancies. Thus, as was initially hypothesized, initiative should mediate the path from resourcefulness to persistence because of the goal-directedness subscale in Ponton's instrument again bearing in mind that the instrument is measuring intention and not motivation directly. This result was partially supported by the path model. However, what was not expected was the nearly equivalent effect of resourcefulness on persistence without the initiative mediator. This may be due to the goal-directedness subscale in Derrick's persistence instrument. If this assumption is correct, then this latter situation may suggest the presence of both forms of cognitive motivation (i.e., expectancy value and goal theories) even without the presence of initiative.

However, if this argument is true, then an *accurate* measure of motivation and self-efficacy (i.e., accurate due to the measures being contextualized to autonomous learning) may change the path coefficients in the overall path-analytic model. Because Meyer's desire instrument is not reflective of such contextual measures, it is presently asserted that such instrumentation should be developed and tested in concert with the conative measures of the LAP. This research will shed better insight into the proposed causal relationships presently argued. In its present form, desire does not accurately measure one's motivation to engage in autonomous learning. Even though the instrument may assess important characteristics of the learner, such an assessment may not accurately reflect one's intention to engage in autonomous learning. Hierarchical linear regression certainly supports the desire instrument's hypothesized lack of predictive ability when the effects of resourcefulness and initiative are controlled.

Concluding Remarks

The present analyses suggest that fostering resourcefulness should be a critical goal in effecting learning persistence. Initiative should be a focus in concert with resourcefulness, but not in isolation;

resourcefulness triggers persistence with an effect size similar to the path with initiative as a mediator.

Significant advances have been made to better understand the characteristics of the adult autonomous learner. Measures of desire, resourcefulness, initiative, and persistence have helped to provide insight into the cognitive, affective, and conative world of the learner. However, to continue on this avenue of research, motivation and self-efficacy instruments should be developed within the context of autonomous learning and tested with the conative measures thereby enabling future research to better describe the relationship between motivation and conation. Hopefully, this understanding will better equip the learning facilitator to not only foster autonomy within learners but also to take fuller advantage of the autonomy that adults tend to exhibit in their learning.

Acknowledgment

The authors would like to thank Gary J. Confessore and EunMi Park for their assistance in acquiring the data analyzed for the present investigation.

References

Atkinson, J. W. (1964). *An introduction to motivation.* Princeton, NJ: D. Van Nostrand.

Atkinson, J. W. (1982). Old and new conceptions of how expected consequences influence action. In N. T. Feather (Ed.), *Expectations and actions: Expectancy-value models in psychology* (pp. 33-49). Hillsdale, NJ: Lawrence Erlbaum Associates.

Bandura, A. (1995). Exercise of personal and collective efficacy in changing societies. In A. Bandura (Ed.), *Self-efficacy in changing societies* (pp. 1-45). Cambridge, UK: Cambridge University Press.

Bandura, A. (1997). *Self-efficacy: The exercise of control.* New York, NY: W. H. Freeman and Company.

Bandura, A., & Cervone, D. (1983). Self-evaluative and self-efficacy mechanisms governing the motivational effects of goal systems. *Journal of Personality and Social Psychology, 45*(5), 1017-1028.

Carr, P. B. (1999). *The measurement of resourcefulness intentions in the adult autonomous learner* (Unpublished doctoral dissertation). The George Washington University, Washington, DC.

Confessore, G. J. (1992). An introduction to the study of self-directed learning. In G. J. Confessore & S. J. Confessore (Eds.), *Guideposts to self-directed learning: Expert commentary on essential concepts* (pp. 1-6). King of Prussia, PA: Organization Design and Development.

Derrick, M. G. (2001). *The measurement of an adult's intention to exhibit persistence in autonomous learning* (Unpublished doctoral dissertation). The George Washington University, Washington, DC.

Derrick, M. G. (2002). Persistence and the adult autonomous learner. In H. B. Long & Associates (Eds.), *Twenty-first century advances in self-directed learning* (pp. 13-30). Schaumburg, IL: Motorola University Press.

Hinkle, D. E., Wiersma, W., & Jurs, S. G. (1998). *Applied statistics for the behavioral sciences* (4th ed.). Boston, MA: Houghton Mifflin.

Locke, E. A., & Latham, G. P. (1990). *A theory of goal setting & task performance.* Englewood Cliffs, NJ: Prentice Hall.

Maxim, P. S. (1999). *Quantitative research methods in the social sciences.* New York, NY: Oxford University Press.

Meyer, D. T. (2001). *The measurement of intentional behavior as a prerequisite to autonomous learning* (Unpublished doctoral dissertation). The George Washington University, Washington, DC.

Park, E., & Confessore, G. J. (2002). Development of new instrumentation: Validation of the Learner Autonomy Profile beta version. In H. B. Long & Associates (Eds.), *Twenty-first century advances in self-directed learning* (pp. 289-306). Schaumburg, IL: Motorola University Press.

Ponton, M. K. (1999). *The measurement of an adult's intention to exhibit personal initiative in autonomous learning* (Unpublished doctoral dissertation). The George Washington University, Washington, DC.

Ponton, M. K., & Carr, P. B. (1999). *A quasi-linear behavioral model and an application to self-directed learning.* (NASA Technical Memorandum 209094). Hampton, VA: NASA Langley Research Center. **[cf. Chapter 1]**

Ponton, M. K., & Carr, P. B. (2000). Understanding and promoting autonomy in self-directed learning. *Current Research in Social Psychology, 5*(19). Retrieved from http://www.uiowa.edu/crisp/ **[cf. Chapter 2]**

Ponton, M. K., & Carr, P. B. (2002). The development of instrumentation that measures an adult's intention to exhibit initiative and resourcefulness in autonomous learning. In H. B. Long & Associates (Eds.), *Twenty-first century advances in self-directed learning* (pp. 223-241). Schaumburg, IL: Motorola University Press.

Ponton, M. K., Edmister, J. H., Ukeiley, L. S., & Seiner, J. M. (2001). Understanding the role of self-efficacy in engineering education. *Journal of Engineering Education, 90*(2), 247-251.

Rosenbaum, M. (1989). Self-control under stress: The role of learned resourcefulness. *Advances in Behaviour Research and Therapy, 11,* 249-258.

Vroom, V. H. (1964). *Work and motivation.* New York, NY: John Wiley and Sons.

Weiner, B. (1985). An attributional theory of achievement motivation and emotion. *Psychological Review, 92*(4), 548-573.

CHAPTER 9

THE RELATIONSHIP BETWEEN RESOURCEFULNESS AND PERSISTENCE IN ADULT AUTONOMOUS LEARNING[9]

The purpose of this study was to investigate the tenability of a proposed path-analytic model relating resourcefulness and persistence in the context of adult autonomous learning. Data collected from a nonprobability sample of 492 American adults using valid and reliable measures for resourcefulness and persistence were analyzed. Results suggest that although adults intend to persist in valued learning activities, they often do not choose to engage in such activities. Methods are discussed that may help educators foster autonomous learning tendencies in their students thereby supporting their development as lifelong learners.

Smith (1982) asserted that *learning* can have several definitions and stated the following:

> Learning is used to refer to (1) the acquisition and mastery of what is already known about something, (2) the extension and clarification of meanings of one's experience, or (3) an organized, intentional process of testing ideas relevant to problems. In other words, it [learning] is used to describe a product, a process, or a function. (p. 34)

In addition, Smith stated that the relevant aspects of the functional perspective include any processes that facilitate learning with an example being the motivation of the learner to engage in intentional change.

Similar to learning, *self-directed learning* has no single definition. Long (1989) provided the assertion that self-directed learning can be viewed along three different dimensions: sociological (addressing the

---

[9]This article is reprinted with permission from *Adult Education Quarterly* and is copyrighted © SAGE [2005, *55*(2), 116-128]

learner's isolation), pedagogical (addressing the learner's activities), and psychological (addressing the learner's mental state). According to Oddi (1987) and Merriam and Caffarella (1999), research conducted within the field of self-directed learning can be grouped into two categories, process or personality characteristic, where the dominant portion of the research has been conducted from the process perspective. The first two dimensions of Long (1989) coincide with the process perspective whereas the third dimension can be viewed from the personality characteristic perspective; however, Long (1998) asserted that only "the *psychological conceptualization* is both necessary and sufficient to explain SDL [self-directed learning]" (p. 10). Long (1998) stated,

> the psychological conceptualization implies that fundamentally learning is a self-initiated, self-directed, and self-regulated cognitive process whereby the learner can choose to ignore instruction, to merely absorb it by casual attention, to carefully memorize without critical reflection, or to seek to change or create an understanding of information. (p. 9)

Knowles (1980) supported the notion that learning processes are predicated on the psychological condition of the learner where "learning is described psychologically as a process of need-meeting and goal-striving by the learners" (p. 56) thereby reinforcing the primacy of understanding the learner's psychological attributes in the study of self-directed learning.

Because of the hypothesized importance of the psychological dimension for self-directed learning and the dearth of research connecting this dimension with concomitant behaviors, recent work focuses on autonomous learning as a manifestation of the learner's autonomy. Ponton (1999) defined learner autonomy as "the characteristic of the person who independently exhibits agency in learning activities" (pp. 13-14) and stated that autonomy represents a subset of the attributes (i.e., agentic actions) associated with self-directedness. The concept of autonomy had been argued previously by both Knowles (1980) and Merriam and Caffarella (1999) as existing within the framework of the learner's attributes whereas Chene (1983) defined learner autonomy in terms of an individual's independence to learn something of value through a process defined at his or her discretion (i.e., a self-defined learning activity). Ponton suggested that learner autonomy is a psychological characteristic within the realm of cognition and affection whereas autonomous learning is the subsequent conative manifestation. The term *conative* is used in conjunction with learner agency because "conation refers to his [i.e., the agent's] behavioral intentions" (Fishbein & Ajzen, 1975, p. 12) and ensuing intentional activity.

Ponton, Carr, and Confessore (2000) have theorized that autonomous learning includes the exhibition of personal initiative, resourcefulness, and persistence in one's learning, and instruments were developed by Ponton (1999), Carr (1999), and Derrick (2001) to measure these three conative factors, respectively. The focus of these investigations was to develop methods to measure behavioral intentions that are coincident with specific cognitive strategies within the domain of adult autonomous learning.

Recent work (Ponton, Carr, & Derrick, 2004) was conducted to determine the tenability of a proposed causal structure with regard to these conative factors. A path analysis was performed on data acquired from a study of 909 adults suggesting that resourcefulness plays a critical role in whether a learner will persist in learning activities. Results indicated that the direct path from resourcefulness to persistence was comparable to the path mediated by initiative. Persistence was modeled as the desired effect because it was asserted to be the defining characteristic of learning that continues to a personally satisfying conclusion. As Derrick (2002) posited, "understanding the behaviors associated with persistence in learning is critical to understanding . . . why some individuals are successful and others are not successful in their learning endeavors" (p. 16). Ponton et al. (2004) argued that if learning facilitators desire to foster perseverant tendencies in autonomous learners, the first step is to foster resourcefulness.

Because of this recent work by Ponton et al. (2004), the motivation behind the present study was to foster a better understanding of the causal relationship between individual resourcefulness subscales and persistence. The ultimate goal of this work and future work is to better enable educators to incorporate instructional strategies that aid in the development of autonomous lifelong learners.

Method

Carr (1999) developed the Inventory of Learner Resourcefulness (ILR); Derrick (2001) developed the Inventory of Learner Persistence (ILP).

The ILR assesses an adult's intention to exhibit the following four behaviors: (a) anticipate the future rewards of present learning, (b) prioritize learning over nonlearning activities, (c) choose learning over nonlearning activities, and (d) solve the problems that interfere with desired learning. The ILP measures the following three behavioral intentions: (a) goal directedness, (b) self-regulation, and (c) volition. Individual items are scored from 0 (*never* applies to the respondent) to 10 (*always* applies to the respondent) where the current Web versions used for the present study offer a 0.25 response resolution. Example items include

ILR

Even if it interferes with my social life, I will choose to learn something because I enjoy learning.

Before I begin a learning activity, I will try to anticipate problems that might interfere with my learning.

ILP

I will consistently work towards achievement of my learning goals no matter how long it may take to accomplish that goal.

I will keep my learning goal my top priority although I have other important things to do.

Carr and Derrick's respective arguments supporting the validity of their respective instruments were based on the development of items with specific theoretical foundations (i.e., construct validity), a review by researchers whose work was pivotal to the development of these theories (i.e., face validity), and the results of principal component analyses performed to support the factor structure of each subscale (i.e., content validity). Since their initial creation, both instruments have undergone three stages of refinement with subsequent validity and reliability analyses. Present versions of the ILR and ILP are licensed by Human Resource Development Enterprises as part of the Learner Autonomy Profile and have been argued as being construct and content valid as well as externally and internally reliable (Park & Confessore, 2002). Previously reported Cronbach's alpha coefficients for each of the subscales are presented in Table 1 (see Park & Confessore, 2002, pp. 296-298). For the present investigation, only the total ILP score (i.e., the summed score of the three ILP subscales) will be considered along with the four ILR subscale scores: these instruments were used in this manner because persistence (i.e., total ILP score) is hypothesized as a desirable end state and dependent on a causal structure of the resourcefulness subscales.

The data from research performed on 492 American adults were analyzed for the present study. These data were aggregated from the results of several smaller investigations conducted by Gary J. Confessore of George Washington University and Eunmi Park of the University of Oklahoma (Confessore and Park have conducted widespread research using the Learner Autonomy Profile on North American, Western European, and East Asian adults). These smaller studies focus on working adults at given consulting sites or on undergraduate/graduate students at given institutions of higher education (i.e., community college or university). Please note that those studied at various consulting sites may also have been students during their off hours. All participants in these investigations completed the Web version of the Learner Autonomy Profile via access to a personal or institutional computer. Because the data for the present investigation do not represent a random sample of the U.S. adult population, generalizability to this population may be a limitation of this study. Data analysis was performed using the SPSS.

Table 1. Internal Reliability (Cronbach's Alpha) for Each Subscale of the ILR and ILP

Subscale	α
ILR subscale	
Anticipate future reward	.89
Prioritize learning over nonlearning	.90
Choose learning over nonlearning	.73
Solve problems that interfere	.93
ILP subscale	
Goal-directedness	.91
Self-regulation	.92
Volition	.92

Note. Park and Confessore (2002, pp. 296-298).

Findings

Sample Demographics

Cross-tabulation of the frequencies associated with gender and highest level of education is presented in Table 2. Note that there were 372 females versus 120 males in the sample and that the majority of the sample did not complete a baccalaureate degree program. The age of the subjects ranged from 17 to 88 years ($M = 37.63$, $SD = 11.64$).

Table 3 presents the descriptive statistics associated with the four ILR resourcefulness subscales and the ILP persistence sum total (i.e., a combination of all three persistence subscales). Note that the mean value varies due to a difference in the number of items associated with each variable measure. Also presented in Table 3 are the skewness and kurtosis statistics for each measure; these statistics suggest that the data are reasonably normal where this assumption is weakest for the subscale prioritizing learning over nonlearning activities.

Table 2. Frequency: Educational Level Versus Gender ($N = 492$)

Highest Education	Female, n	Male, n	Total
High School Diploma	236	47	283
Baccalaureate Degree	68	16	84
Graduate/Professional Degree	68	57	125

Table 3. Descriptive Statistics for the ILR Subscales and the ILP ($N = 492$)

Variable	M	SD	Skewness	Kurtosis
ILR subscale				
Anticipate future rewards	86.43	15.84	-.706	-.157
Prioritize learning over nonlearning	85.90	12.27	-1.233	1.421
Choose learning over nonlearning	68.74	15.20	-.089	-.533
Solve problems that interfere	172.30	30.09	-.629	-.143
ILP total	277.50	42.79	-.917	.795

Proposed Causal Model

As indicated in Table 4, a statistically significant ($p < .001$) linear relationship exists between all five variables. According to Hinkle, Wiersma, and Jurs (1998, p. 120), all correlations can be described qualitatively from moderate ($.5 < r < .7$) to high ($.7 < r < .9$). The presence of significant linear relationships suggests that the use of linear techniques in analyzing the data is appropriate.

Table 4. Intercorrelations Using ILR Subscales and the ILP Total ($N = 492$)

Variable	1	2	3	4	5
ILR subscales					
1. Anticipate future rewards	—	.796**	.569**	.876**	.796**
2. Prioritize learning over nonlearning		—	.612**	.830**	.789**
3. Choose learning over nonlearning			—	.569**	.573**
4. Solve problems that interfere				—	.838**
5. ILP total					—

**$p < .001$.

Expectancy value theory suggests that individuals are motivated to engage in pursuits that will either lead to personally valued outcomes or avoid aversive outcomes (Bandura, 1997: Vroom, 1964). Bandura (1997) suggested that outcomes can take three major forms: physical (e.g., pleasure, pain), social (e.g., approval, recognition, money, rejection, sanctions), and self-evaluative. Self-evaluative outcomes represent reactions to one's behavior as compared to self-standards of personally defined correct behavior. Once personal values are formed, behaviors are selected and performance goals established by the agent for activities in which the agent feels efficacious (i.e., perceives the presence of personal capability required for a successful performance) and believes will lead to a desirable end state. Strong efficacy beliefs influence not only activity choice but also the degree to which goals are pursued in spite of the presence of obstacles (Bandura, 1997).

Because outcome expectancies precede activity choice and goal creation, it has been previously hypothesized that the anticipation of future rewards will influence an agent to prioritize learning over nonlearning activities and, thus, choose learning over nonlearning activities (Ponton et al., 2004). It is presently asserted that solving the problems that interfere with learning will occur only after learning is a choice activity. Performance of these four subscales is hypothesized to lead to persistence in the following causal path:

Anticipate Future Rewards → Prioritize Learning Over Nonlearning → Choose Learning Over Nonlearning → Solve Problems That Interfere With Learning → Persistence

In addition, it is also presently hypothesized that anticipating future rewards should have a minimal direct effect on persistence when compared to the indirect effect of the above causal path. This is because other ILR subscales are posited as being essential factors in the enactment of learning persistence.

Findings

Path coefficients were determined using the coefficients from the following series of standardized linear regression equations (Maxim, 1999) based on the hypothesized model:

$$z_{\hat{P}} = p_{PA}z_A + p_{PP_R}z_{P_R} + p_{PC}z_C + p_{PS}z_S ,$$

$$z_{\hat{S}} = p_{SC}z_C ,$$

$$z_{\hat{C}} = p_{CP_R}z_{P_R} ,$$

$$z_{\hat{P}_R} = p_{P_RA}z_A .$$

Note that A, P_R, C, S, and P correspond to anticipate future rewards, prioritize learning over nonlearning activities, choose learning over nonlearning activities, solve problems that interfere with learning, and persistence, respectively. The resulting path-analytic model is presented in Figure 1. All path coefficients are statistically significant at the .01 level. This model presents four paths from anticipate future rewards to persistence: one direct effect ($A \rightarrow P$) and three indirect effects ($A \rightarrow$

$P_R \rightarrow P$, $A \rightarrow P_R \rightarrow C \rightarrow P$, and $A \rightarrow P_R \rightarrow C \rightarrow S \rightarrow P$). The effect sizes for these four paths are presented in Table 5.

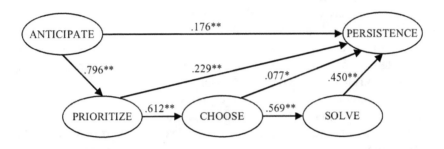

Figure 1. Overall path-analytic model: Influence of the four resourcefulness subscales on persistence.
$*p = .01$; $**p < .001$.

Contrary to the two research hypotheses, the indirect path $A \rightarrow P_R \rightarrow C \rightarrow S \rightarrow P$ is not the largest path to persistence and the direct path $A \rightarrow P$ is not small in comparison (in fact, it is larger). The largest path is $A \rightarrow P_R \rightarrow P$ with the direct path $A \rightarrow P$ comparable in magnitude; however, the total indirect effect is approximately twice as large as the direct effect thus suggesting the importance of understanding the indirect paths.

Table 5. Effect Sizes for Different Paths in the Path-Analytic Model

Path	Effect Size
$A \rightarrow P$	.176
$A \rightarrow P_R \rightarrow P$	$(.796)(.229) = .182$
$A \rightarrow P_R \rightarrow C \rightarrow P$	$(.796)(.612)(.077) = .0375$
$A \rightarrow P_R \rightarrow C \rightarrow S \rightarrow P$	$(.796)(.612)(.569)(.450) = .125$

Note. The total indirect effect is $.182 + .0375 + .125 = .345$.
Symbol key: A = anticipate future rewards, P_R = prioritize learning over nonlearning, C = choose learning over nonlearning, S = solve problems that interfere, and P = persistence; A, P_R, C, and S are ILR subscale scores while P is the ILP total score.

Discussion

In higher education, persistence usually refers to a continuance of study to degree completion within some prescribed time period (e.g., 6 years). Obviously, it is difficult to understand how one may be persistent in any endeavor unless one chooses to engage in that endeavor over other activities. Unfortunately, this concept of persistence may not adequately describe an adult's persistence in autonomous learning as defined by Derrick (2001).

The path-analytic model of the present investigation suggests that an adult's persistence in autonomous learning is more related to the anticipation of future rewards of present learning, with or without the mediating influence of prioritizing learning over nonlearning activities, than with the mediating effect of choosing of learning over nonlearning activities. Note that previously, persistence was defined by Derrick (2001) as one's intention to exhibit goal directedness, self-regulation, and volition in one's learning. What does this mean for an adult to exhibit persistence in learning, as defined by Derrick, but not necessarily choose to engage in learning as opposed to nonlearning activities?

This may reflect the nature of adulthood. Without question, an adult has multiple life roles (e.g., spouse, parent, worker, or friend) with their associated exigencies. Although an adult may anticipate the future rewards of present learning and even prioritize such learning over nonlearning activities in terms of value attribution, the lawn may need mowing, the kids may need to be taken to soccer practice, or perhaps a friend may need consoling now. This does not mean that valued learning activities are not still within the agent's mind and that associated cognitive activities (i.e., goal directedness, self-regulation, and volition) are still intended behaviors (recall that the ILP assesses behavioral intentions); however, it does mean that an adult must often choose other activities based on a multitude of responsibilities. In terms of value to a particular adult's long term development, learning may still be the most highly prized activity, but the roof may need fixing today (as an example).

The exhibition of autonomy is presently argued as domain specific. That is, one can be an autonomous lawn mower or an autonomous learner. If one anticipates the future rewards of cutting the grass, prioritizes cutting the grass over other activities, chooses to cut the grass over other activities, and solves problems associated with cutting the grass then one is exhibiting resourcefulness in lawn mowing due to resourcefulness being defined as a behavioral syndrome (i.e., co-occurring behaviors; Carr, 1999). Similarly, when all of the subscale intentions associated with initiative and persistence are exhibited in addition to resourcefulness, then one may be deemed an autonomous lawn mower. However, because choices are made with respect to activities that vie for one's time and energy, if one has tendencies to exhibit autonomy in domains other than learning, then one will not be an autonomous learner. Thus, although the present results suggest what adults may actually do (at least within the limitations of generalizability), these results also suggest that statistically, the researched sample does not represent autonomous learners because choosing learning is not part of the dominant two paths. Intentions associated with persistence in learning may be exhibited, but learning activities may not be completed quickly due to participation in other activities. Derrick's (2001) model of persistence represents a set of cognitive strategies rather than temporal deadlines.

Because the intent of this study was to provide insight that may help the development of autonomous lifelong learners, it is important to discuss facilitative strategies that may foster choosing learning over nonlearning activities. The reality is that not all nonlearning activities are emergencies as previously highlighted. As per the path analytic model, when adults do choose learning over nonlearning activities, the path $A \rightarrow P_R \rightarrow C \rightarrow S \rightarrow P$ is close in magnitude (indirect effect = .125) to $A \rightarrow P$ (direct effect = .176) and $A \rightarrow P_R \rightarrow P$ (indirect effect = .182), albeit slightly smaller. This suggests that when adults do choose learning over nonlearning activities, they also must solve the problems that impede desired levels of learning (e.g., gather needed learning resources). Thus, the present issue is defining potential methods that an educator can invoke to help the learner develop a tendency to choose learning activities over nonlearning activities.

One hypothesized method is to help the learner become aware that choices are being made in lieu of desirable learning activities. Educators may require students to keep a log of the following for some fixed time period (e.g., 1 week): (a) desired learning activities for the period (recorded at the beginning of the period); (b) the anticipated benefits of participating in the desired learning activities (recorded at the beginning of the period); (c) each activity chosen throughout the period (recorded before commencing each activity); (d) what value, both short- and long-term, was anticipated in choosing the activity (recorded before commencing); (e) if the activity was a nonlearning activity, why the anticipated benefits of the activity were more important than those anticipated for the desired learning activities (recorded before commencing); (f) the duration of the activity; (g) if the activity was a nonlearning activity, a comparison between the benefits realized and the anticipated benefits of the desired learning activities for the period (recorded after completing the activity); if the activity was a learning activity, a comparison between anticipated and realized benefits; and (h) a synopsis of the period's activities addressing the time spent in various activities and the benefits realized (recorded at the end of the period). The intent of this process is to foster an awareness of the implications of activity choices with respect to both time and value; self-monitoring processes have been argued as being an important mechanism in developing self-regulated learners (Zimmerman, Bonner, & Kovach, 1996).

To facilitate this journaling activity, an educator may need to help students assess value from a learning perspective. Houle (1961) suggested that adult learners are motivated to participate in learning activities because (a) such activities are a means to accomplish specific goals, (b) seeking knowledge is personally gratifying, and (c) such activities are socially gratifying; goal oriented, learning oriented, and activity oriented, respectively, as characterized by Houle. Heckhausen and Kuhl (1985) "define[d] [a] goal as the molar endstate whose attainment requires actions by the individual pursuing it" (pp. 137-138); thus, in a general sense, goal-oriented, learning-oriented, and activity-oriented learners are all goal-directed agents where the nature of the goals varies. Heckhausen and Kuhl further stated that "goals rest on three levels of endstates with an ascending hierarchical order" (p. 138) and are described as follows:

> On the first-order level the endstates are the activities themselves: the interest in, or the enjoyment of, doing something repetitively or continuously, because it provides excitement. . . . On a second-order level the endstate is an action outcome with characteristics that are required or preset and that are inherently valuable. Finally, at the third-order level, the endstate refers to desirable consequences that might arise from an achieved outcome. (p. 138)

These three levels of end states are congruent with Houle's triumvirate and should be used by facilitators to help students to identify the potential and actual benefits associated with participating in learning activities.

If an adult truly values learning, an active consideration of this valuation during periods of discretionary time may lead to choosing learning over nonlearning activities. From a purely agentic perspective, classifying activities as either time spent or time wasted is an important cognitive activity that empowers an individual to select activities that promote self-fulfilling lives within the framework of a personal value system. This process may help learners to not interpret choosing learning over nonlearning activities as a delay in gratification but rather as immediate gratification because of the eventual valued outcomes anticipated.

Another hypothesized strategy to facilitate autonomous learning is to reinforce a self-identification by students as being continual learners. The activities in which people engage themselves are related to how they see themselves (Kuhl & Fuhrmann, 1998). Thus, if one believes himself or herself to be someone who is actively and continually learning new things that add meaning and quality to life, then one may choose to participate in learning activities that reinforce this self-image and avoid activities that are inconsistent with this image. Adult educators, by definition, are dealing with adults who are participating in a learning activity; therefore, supporting this self-image is consistent with the evidence provided. Helping students to identify themselves as lifelong learners may facilitate choosing learning activities that are coincident with this ingrained self-image.

Concluding Remarks

The results presented suggest that although adults may intend on exhibiting persistent behaviors in their learning activities, they may not actually choose learning over nonlearning activities. Adults that anticipate the future rewards of learning, perhaps mediated by prioritizing learning over nonlearning activities, exhibit the intentions to persist in their learning as defined by Derrick (2001) as goal directedness, self-regulation, and volition. However, the limited results of the present study suggest that even with these value attributions, the path to persistence is not mediated by choosing to engage in desired learning activities. When they do choose learning activities, however, their persistence is mediated by solving the problems that interfere with desired levels of learning.

To foster autonomous learning tendencies (i.e., help students to choose learning over nonlearning activities), it is hypothesized that educators should help students to increase their awareness of the implications of activity choices (e.g., time investment, outcome assessment) through active self-monitoring. Also, because activity choice is related to self-image, educators should reinforce their students' definition of themselves as continual, lifelong learners so that future learning activities are chosen to reinforce this ingrained self-image. Although consistent with theory, these strategies should be empirically tested for their effectiveness on fostering autonomous learning.

Learning activities are able to transform lives only if a learner chooses to engage in such activities. The mere recognition of the importance of such activities followed by an intention to persist does not serve any developmental role for the nonparticipant. However, if educators can help students to transform into continual, lifelong learners who are armed with the cognitive strategies required to choose learning over nonlearning activities, then these learners are well on their way to autonomously make choices that may direct life trajectories in personally satisfying directions. Such empowerment over one's life course is the true value of formal education.

References

Bandura, A. (1997). *Self-efficacy: The exercise of control*. New York, NY: W. H. Freeman and Company.

Carr, P. B. (1999). *The measurement of resourcefulness intentions in the adult autonomous learner* (Unpublished doctoral dissertation). The George Washington University, Washington, DC.

Chene, A. (1983). The concept of autonomy in adult education: A philosophical discussion. *Adult Education Quarterly, 34*(1), 38-47.

Derrick, M. G. (2001). *The measurement of an adult's intention to exhibit persistence in autonomous learning* (Unpublished doctoral dissertation). The George Washington University, Washington, DC.

Derrick, M. G. (2002). Persistence and the adult autonomous learner. In H. B. Long & Associates (Eds.), *Twenty-first century advances in self-directed learning* (pp. 13-30). Schaumburg, IL: Motorola University Press.

Fishbein, M., & Ajzen. I. (1975). *Belief, attitude, intention, and behavior: An introduction to theory and research*. Reading. MA: Addison-Wesley.

Heckhausen, H., & Kuhl, J. (1985). From wishes to action: The dead ends and short cuts on the long way to action. In M. Frese & J. Sabini (Eds.), *Goal-directed behavior: The concept of action in psychology* (pp. 134-157). Hillsdale, NJ: Lawrence Erlbaum.

Hinkle, D. E., Wiersma, W., & Jurs, S. G. (1998). *Applied statistics for the behavioral sciences* (4th ed.). Boston, MA: Houghton Mifflin.

Houle, C. O. (1961). *The inquiring mind: A study of the adult who continues to learn*. Madison, WI: University of Wisconsin Press.

Knowles, M. S. (1980). *The modern practice of adult education: From pedagogy to andragogy*. New York, NY: Cambridge Books.

Kuhl. J., & Fuhrmann, A. (1998). Decomposing self-regulation and self-control: The Volitional Components Inventory. In J. Heckhausen & C. S. Dweck (Eds.), *Motivation and self-regulation across the life span* (pp. 15-49). Cambridge, UK: Cambridge University Press.

Long, H. B. (1989). Self-directed learning: Emerging theory and practice. In H. B. Long & Associates (Eds.), *Self-directed learning: Emerging theory and practice* (pp. 1-11). Norman: University of Oklahoma, Oklahoma Research Center for Continuing Professional and Higher Education.

Long, H. B. (1998). Theoretical and practical implications of selected paradigms of self-directed learning. In H. B. Long & Associates (Eds.), *Developing paradigms for self-directed learning* (pp. 1-14). Norman: University of Oklahoma, Public Managers Center, College of Education.

Maxim, P. S. (1999). *Quantitative research methods in the social sciences*. New York, NY: Oxford University Press.

Merriam, S. B., & Caffarella, R. S. (1999). *Learning in adulthood: A comprehensive guide* (2nd ed.). San Francisco, CA: Jossey-Bass.

Oddi, L. F. (1987). Perspective on self-directed learning. *Adult Education Quarterly, 38*(1), 21-31.

Park, E., & Confessore, G. J. (2002). Development of new instrumentation: Validation of the Learner Autonomy Profile beta version. In H. B. Long & Associates (Eds.), *Twenty-first century advances in self-directed learning* (pp. 289-306). Schaumburg, IL: Motorola University Press.

Ponton, M. K. (1999). *The measurement of an adult's intention to exhibit personal initiative in autonomous learning* (Unpublished doctoral dissertation). The George Washington University, Washington, DC.

Ponton, M. K., Carr, P. B., & Confessore, G. J. (2000). Learning conation: A psychological perspective of personal initiative and resourcefulness. In H. B. Long & Associates (Eds.), *Practice & theory in self-directed learning* (pp. 65-82). Schaumburg, IL: Motorola University Press.

Ponton, M. K., Carr, P. B., & Derrick, M. G. (2004). A path analysis of the conative factors associated with autonomous learning. *International Journal of Self-Directed Learning, 1,* 59-69. **[cf. Chapter 8]**

Smith, R. M. (1982). *Learning how to learn: Applied theory for adults.* Chicago, IL: Follett.

Vroom, V. H. (1964). *Work and motivation.* New York, NY: John Wiley and Sons.

Zimmerman, B. J., Bonner, S., & Kovach, R. (1996). *Developing self-regulated learners: Beyond achievement to self-efficacy.* Washington, DC: American Psychological Association.

CHAPTER 10

THE ROLE OF SELF-EFFICACY IN AUTONOMOUS LEARNING[10]

The purpose of this correlational study was to investigate the relationship of self-efficacy with other factors associated with autonomous learning (i.e., desire, resourcefulness, initiative, and persistence). Five instruments were administered to a nonprobability sample of 82 adults: the Inventory of Learner Desire, the Inventory of Learner Resourcefulness, the Inventory of Learner Initiative, the Inventory of Learner Persistence, and the Appraisal of Learner Autonomy (i.e., a self-efficacy scale). The results suggest that self-efficacy does not mediate the relationship between desire and autonomous learning as suggested by a previously hypothesized path analytic model; however, self-efficacy does account for variance in autonomous learning unexplained by desire. Thus, the theorized four sources of efficacy information should be considered in facilitating autonomous learning tendencies. Motivational measures contextualized to autonomous learning are needed to more adequately test the mediating role of self-efficacy.

In 1999, Ponton offered a definition of *learner autonomy* as "the characteristic of the person who independently exhibits agency [i.e., intentional behavior] in learning activities" (pp. 13-14). He asserted that autonomy represents a subset of the cognitive and affective characteristics of the agent under a larger set associated with self-directedness (i.e., autonomy is a less restrictive categorization). In contrast to learner autonomy, Ponton suggested that *autonomous learning* refers to the conative manifestations of extant learner autonomy and is a subset of all manifestations associated with self-directed learning. The term "conative" is used with aspects of autonomous learning because "conation refers to his [sic, i.e., the

---

[10]This article is reprinted with permission from the *International Journal for Self-Directed Learning* (http://sdlglobal.com/journals.php) and is copyrighted © The International Society for Self-Directed Learning [2005, *2*(2), 81-90]

agent's] behavioral intentions" (Fishbein & Ajzen, 1975, p. 12) and subsequent intentional action.

Over the past 6 years researchers have focused on the development of instrumentation relevant to autonomous learning. Such instrumentation include the Inventory of Learner Desire (ILD; cf. Meyer, 2001), the Inventory of Learner Resourcefulness (ILR; Carr, 1999), the Inventory of Learner Initiative (ILI; Ponton, 1999), and the Inventory of Learner Persistence (ILP; Derrick, 2001). The motivation behind focusing on the four conative factors of desire, resourcefulness, initiative, and persistence was based upon earlier work by Confessore (1992) who emphasized the importance of their manifestation in personally satisfying self-directed learning endeavors. A study of these four factors is conceptualized as necessary but not sufficient in understanding autonomous learning. While desire is a cognitive/affective characteristic of the agent, resourcefulness, initiative, and persistence represent conative manifestations (Ponton & Carr, 2000). Each of these instruments has been continually refined and analyzed to support validity and reliability (cf. Confessore & Park, 2004).

In addition to the four instruments highlighted, Ponton, Carr, and Derrick (2003) suggested that a measure of self-efficacy in autonomous learning was also needed "to better describe the relationship between motivation and conation" (p. 13). Self-efficacy is the belief that capability exists to successfully execute a given performance. Citing research in multiple domains of human functioning, Bandura (1997) offered a compelling argument that self efficacy provides an important mediating role in understanding the relationship between motivation and agency (i.e., intentional acts): that is, valued outcomes or related performance goals will not provide motivation unless the agent believes that requisite capability exists for successful attainments. Ponton et al. asserted that Meyer's measure of desire may have limited explanatory power with respect to autonomous learning because the instrument was designed to measure the extent to which an individual feels able to act intentionally where such intentional action may or may not be manifest as autonomous learning (i.e., Meyer's instrument is not contextualized to autonomous learning while the other three instruments are). Thus, the study of self-efficacy may provide additional explanatory power in understanding and facilitating autonomous learning.

In 2004, Ponton, Derrick, Carr, and Hall developed the Appraisal of Learner Autonomy (ALA) as a measure of self-efficacy in autonomous learning. Methods outlined by Bandura (2001) were followed in developing the ALA. Analysis performed on data acquired from two separate pilot studies resulted in a 9-item instrument that was argued as valid and reliable. Using self-efficacy theory, Ponton et al. hypothesized that self-efficacy (ALA) should mediate the path from desire (ILD) to autonomous learning conation (ILR+ILI+ILP). The purpose of the present study was to investigate this hypothesis and the relationship between self-efficacy and autonomous learning conation.

Methodology

A nonprobability sample of 82 adults were administered the ILD, ILR, ILI, ILP, and ALA as a battery associated with the online version of the Learner Autonomy Profile (LAP; licensed to Human Resource Development Enterprises). Institutional Review Board approval was obtained for this study from the data acquiring investigators respective universities (i.e., Regent University and The George Washington University). The majority of the participants were doctoral students while others were participants in ancillary research investigations. Because the sample does not represent a random sample of the adult population, generalization of results should be performed cautiously.

The demographics of the sample are presented in Table 1. The majority of the participants were female (P = 78%) and had a graduate degree (P = 56%). The average age of the sample was 35.65 years (SD = 8.28) and ranged from 23 to 56 years.

Table 1: Sample Demographics (N = 82)

Variable	n
Gender	
Male	18
Female	64
Highest Educational Attainment	
High School Diploma	2
Bachelor's Degree	34
Graduate Degree	46

Note. The age range of the participants was 23-56 (M = 35.65, SD = 8.28).

Appraisal of Learner Autonomy

The recent development and limited usage of the ALA motivated the authors to conduct additional analysis supporting the instrument's content validity (i.e., item homogeneity); therefore, results from a principal component analysis are presented for the ALA but not the other scales used. Correlation analyses are subsequently presented for all scales in the results section.

All items associated with the ALA support the overall construct of self-efficacy in autonomous learning; therefore, item homogeneity is hypothesized to exist. Gorsuch (1983) asserted that the first principal component represents the best condensation of a group of variables; thus, this form of analysis was conducted to uncover uncorrelated (i.e., orthogonal) common factors where each factor sequentially accounts for the maximum remaining variance in the instrument's items (Dunteman, 1989).

The analysis performed was on the correlation matrix and may be dependent upon sampling variability (Kim & Mueller, 1978) thus suggesting the importance of an adequate sample size. Kline (1993) suggested a minimum subject-to-item ratio of 2:1 (p. 121) although he asserted that such rules-of-thumb vary greatly between researchers. However, because the sample size to item number was approximately 9:1 (i.e., 82:9), the sample size was assumed to be sufficient for the principal component analysis performed.

The Kaiser-Meyer-Olkin Measure of Sampling Adequacy (MSA) and the Bartlett Test of Sphericity were used to assess the suitability of the correlation matrix for factor analysis. For factor analysis, the MSA index should be no less than 0.5 (Cureton & D'Agostino, 1983, p. 389) and Bartlett's χ^2 should enable a rejection of the null hypothesis of no difference between the correlation matrix and the identity matrix (Norusis, 1988); that is, common factors cannot exist unless partial correlations between the items exist. As presented in Table 2, MSA = 0.86 and Bartlett's $\chi^2(36, N = 82) = 312.86$ with $p < 0.001$; thus, the sample was assumed adequate for principal component analysis. Gorsuch (1983) asserted that a minimum factor loading of 0.3 (p. 210) is a generally accepted criterion in identifying relevant item loadings. The results presented in Table 2 indicate that all nine items load above this criterion (minimum loading is 0.507) thereby supporting item homogeneity.

Table 2: Principal Component Analysis of the ALA

Item	Factor Loading
1	0.698
2	0.656
3	0.507
4	0.777
5	0.784
6	0.715
7	0.752
8	0.637
9	0.837

Note. First component explaining 50.85% of the total variance. Kaiser-Meyer-Olkin Measure of Sampling Adequacy (MSA) = 0.86; Bartlett's Test of Sphericity approximate $\chi^2(36, N = 82) = 312.86, p < 0.001$.

Reliability

Cronbach's alpha coefficient was computed as a measure of internal consistency for all scales used. In general, the alpha coefficient should be no less than 0.7 (Kline, 1993, p. 11). As is evident in Table 3, internal consistency is tenable for all scales.

Table 3: Internal Reliability (Cronbach's Alpha) for Each Scale

Scale	α
Inventory of Learner Desire	0.95
Inventory of Learner Resourcefulness	0.97
Inventory of Learner Initiative	0.96
Inventory of Learner Persistence	0.98
Appraisal of Learner Autonomy	0.87

Findings

Table 4 presents the Pearson product moment correlations for all variables measured. Excluding self-efficacy, all correlations are moderate to high (qualitative description according to Hinkle, Wiersma, & Jurs, 1998, p. 120), positive, and statistically significant at the 0.001 level. Self-efficacy has a low positive correlation with all variables ($p < .01$) except for the nonsignificant correlation with desire. The correlation between desire and autonomous learning (i.e., ILR+ILI+ILP) is $r = 0.712$ ($p < .001$) while the correlation between self-efficacy and autonomous learning is $r = 0.399$ ($p < .001$).

Table 4: Intercorrelations Between Variables

Variable	1	2	3	4	5
1. Desire	-	0.69**	0.66**	0.71**	0.14
2. Resourcefulness		-	0.89**	0.87**	0.35*
3. Initiative			-	0.89**	0.41**
4. Persistence				-	0.40**
5. Self-Efficacy					-

$*p = .001; **p < .001.$

Because of the lack of a statistically significant correlation between desire and self-efficacy, the hypothesized path model (i.e., desire → self-efficacy → autonomous learning) is untenable; however, this nonsignificant correlation coupled with the significant correlations between desire and self-efficacy with autonomous learning suggest that desire and self-efficacy explain unique variance in autonomous learning. Thus, a regression analysis was performed (see Table 5). Considering each independent variable separately, desire accounts for more of the variance in autonomous learning ($R^2 = 50.7\%$) than does self-efficacy ($R^2 = 15.9\%$); however, together desire and self-efficacy account for 59.7% of the variance in autonomous learning. Adding self-efficacy in Step 2 of the stepwise procedure increases R^2 by 8.9%, which is a significant change at the .001 level.

Table 5: Summary of Hierarchical Regression Analysis for Variables
Predicting Autonomous Learning

Variable	B	$SE\ B$	β
Step 1a			
Desire	2.704	0.298	0.712**
Step 1b			
Self-Efficacy	0.492	0.126	0.399**
Step 2			
Desire	2.539	0.274	0.669**
Self-Efficacy	0.373	0.089	0.302**

Note. $R^2 = .507$ for Step 1a; $R^2 = .159$ for Step 1b; $\Delta R^2 = .089$ from Step 1a to Step 2 ($p < .001$ for change).
**$p < .001$.

Discussion

Mediating Role of Self-Efficacy

The first purpose of this study was to test the hypothesis that self-efficacy mediates the path from desire to autonomous learning (Ponton et al., 2004); however, the lack of correlation presently measured between desire and self-efficacy suggests that this hypothesis is untenable.

According to social cognitive theory (Bandura, 1997), much of human motivation is cognitively induced. Based upon value attributions of expected outcomes associated with an array of possible activities, favorable courses of action are chosen. Such courses include not only action plans but also specific performance goals that serve as indicators of achievement. Even somatically related performances, like eating, may be motivated by cognitive activity rather than cellular deficiency, an example being eating due to the availability of an anticipated satisfying dish rather than due to hunger.

In general, humans do not engage in activities that are self-perceived as futile. To accomplish valued outcomes or avoid aversive ones, activities are chosen due to beliefs of efficacy. Engaging in activities that one believes cannot be performed successfully is a waste of time and energy as other courses of action that are within the efficacious range of the agent are more attractive. Note that self-efficacy is a perception as actual capability can exist even if not perceived to exist; however, it is the perception that affects activity choice and ultimate levels achievement (Bandura, 1997).

Self-efficacy is a domain specific assessment. For example, a self-perception of tennis capability can be decidedly different than a self-perception of calculus capability. Therefore, measures of self-efficacy must be contextualized to the specific activity being assessed. Generalized measures of self-efficacy provide little predictive utility beyond what trait theories might suggest. A reasonable assertion may also be that measures of motivation should be domain specific as well. To make a general statement that *a person is motivated* makes little sense in understanding that person's commitment to engage in specific activities such as activity X versus activity Y; more relevant measures would address the levels of motivation present to engage in either activity X or activity Y. If a person is interested in engaging in activity X due to expected valued outcomes and if a sufficient level of self-efficacy is present with respect to activity X, then the person may actually be motivated to choose to engage in activity X and persevere to satisfying levels of attainment; this simple example essentially describes the mediating role of self-efficacy between motivational considerations and conation.

In the present study, desire was used as the measure of motivation in testing the previously hypothesized mediating role of self-efficacy (Ponton et al., 2004). In general, Meyer's (2001) instrument is a measure of freedom, power, and change; that is, the precursors to intention formation (Confessore & Park, 2004). However, Meyer's instrument is not contextualized to the domain of autonomous learning, which may explain why the path analytic model is not supported by the present results. To more adequately test the previously hypothesized path analytic model, instrumentation must be developed that measures an agent's motivation to engage in autonomous learning. Such an instrument would measure outcome expectancies, goals, and causal attributions associated with showing resourcefulness, initiative, and persistence in one's learning.

The need for such a motivational instrument should not be interpreted as marginalizing the role of Meyer's measure of desire as the ILD consistently has provided moderate to high correlations with the ILR, ILI, and ILP in several previous studies thus supporting its predictive utility. In addition, the theoretical foundation upon which the ILD was developed does provide a degree of explanatory power as well because the level to which a person believes he or she can act intentionally should affect autonomous participation in many domains of human functioning. However, to fully assess the presence of learner autonomy where both motivation and self-efficacy reside, instrumentation should focus on the specific domain of autonomous learning.

It should be noted that *showing* resourcefulness, initiative, and persistence in one's learning is conceptually separable from what is measured in the present study. The ILR, ILI, and ILP are measures of *intention to show* resourcefulness, initiative, and persistence. These instruments were developed in this manner because it is not possible to know, a priori, whether or not study participants are currently engaged in autonomous learning activities (cf. Ponton, 1999). Further research is necessary to uncover the strength of the relationship between the intention to engage in autonomous learning and the enactment of the behaviors of autonomous learning, the latter being the exhibition of resourcefulness, initiative, and persistence.

Correlational Role of Self-Efficacy

As a single independent variable, self-efficacy is associated with 15.9% of the variance in the dependent variable autonomous learning where autonomous learning is the summation of ILR, ILI, and ILP scores; in a stepwise regression procedure, self-efficacy (i.e., Step 2) explains 8.9% ($p < .001$) additional variance in autonomous learning after desire (i.e., Step 1). These results suggest that self-efficacy is significantly related to autonomous learning in a predictive sense. Due to its theoretical foundations and focus on autonomous learning, self-efficacy also provides explanatory power.

A major goal of research is not just the development of theory but using theory to inform practice. Thus, it is not sufficient to merely understand the variables associated with learner autonomy or autonomous learning but rather to use such knowledge in identifying facilitative schemes. Fortunately, social cognitive theory outlines four sources of efficacy information (Bandura, 1997) that should be addressed by autonomous learning facilitators. These sources are mastery experiences, verbal persuasion, vicarious experiences, and physiological/emotive arousals.

In order for learners to feel capable of engaging in autonomous learning, they must have mastery experiences. That is, they must have authentic learning experiences that require the exhibition of resourcefulness, initiative, and persistence in reaching satisfying levels of learning. To promote autonomy (where beliefs of efficacy reside), facilitators should create opportunities for autonomous learning to occur. Of course it is incumbent upon the facilitator to identify appropriate requirements for a learner's level of autonomy; however, there is no reason that activities requiring autonomous learning cannot be incorporated even at very early stages of education provided that requisite learning skills (e.g., reading, acquiring information) are present. Formal education should be based upon the notion that students are assisted in developing their autonomy through progressively structured mastery experiences that require increasing exhibitions of autonomous learning. Through successful learning endeavors and attributing such successes to personal autonomy, beliefs in self-efficacy with respect to autonomous learning capability can be strengthened.

However, if the learner attributes success to factors other than personal capability, self-efficacy may not be enhanced. Thus, the facilitator should use verbal persuasion to inform the learner that success in autonomous learning endeavors is due to individual autonomy rather than facilitative opportunities. Provided the facilitator's opinion is valued by the learner, such persuasions can serve to enhance self-efficacy.

Initially motivating engagement in autonomous learning activities may provide discomfort particularly when high levels of autonomy have not been required in past endeavors. From a motivational perspective, the facilitator should articulate the advantages of being an autonomous learner not only in satisfying proximal course goals and successful program completion but also from the distal perspective of personal empowerment via lifelong learning. Facilitators should help learners to interpret feelings of discomfort (i.e., physiological/emotive arousals) as merely temporary responses due to engaging in unfamiliar activities rather than as indicants of incapability. In addition, providing evidence of similar others who were successful in autonomous learning tasks can provide vicarious experiences that strengthen efficacy as well; thoughts of "if a person like me has done it, perhaps I can do it as well" increase self-perceptions that success due to personal capability is possible.

If these four sources of efficacy information are considered, a facilitator can structure learning activities and interpersonal interactions in a manner that strengthen the learner's self-efficacy. Coupled with the motivation to engage in autonomous learning activities, a strong sense of efficacy will promote an agent's selection of such activities as well as the subsequent perseverance required to overcome obstacles that interfere with attaining desired levels of learning. To exhibit resourcefulness, initiative, and persistence in learning requires the agent to believe that he or she *can* exhibit these conative factors.

Concluding Remarks

The Inventory of Learner Desire may be an inadequate measure of an individual's motivation to engage in autonomous learning activities due to the lack of correlation between desire and self-efficacy. It is presently argued that an adequate motivation instrument should be contextualized to autonomous learning, similar to domain specific self-efficacy scales. Thus, the instrument should be designed to assess the motivation to show resourcefulness, initiative, and persistence in one's learning.

There are many as yet unidentified variables that will constitute the constellation of factors associated with learner autonomy; however, the present study suggests that self-efficacy in autonomous learning must be included in this set. Because of its importance, persons interested in facilitating the development of learner autonomy must consider the sources of efficacy information (i.e., mastery experiences, verbal persuasion, vicarious experiences, and physiological/emotive arousals) in structuring learning activities so that such activities strengthen efficacy beliefs.

This does not mean that self-efficacy is the sole determinant of an agent's engagement in autonomous learning activities (i.e., activities that require personal resourcefulness, initiative, and persistence). According to expectancy value theory and goal theory, respectively, such activities must also be perceived as leading to valued outcomes and adopted performance goals should be perceived as correlated to these outcomes. With continued study and instrument development, the impact of motivation in autonomous learning as well as the ability of other factors to explain the variance in autonomous learning will be better understood. While current conceptualizations of both learner autonomy and autonomous learning have led to a refined understanding of psychological factors associated with adult learning, future work will enable facilitators at all levels of education to maximally develop lifelong learners.

References

Bandura, A. (1997). *Self-efficacy: The exercise of control.* New York, NY: W. H. Freeman and Company.

Bandura, A. (2001). *Guide for constructing self-efficacy scales.* Unpublished manuscript, Department of Psychology, Stanford University, Stanford, CA.

Carr, P. B. (1999). *The measurement of resourcefulness intentions in the adult autonomous learner* (Unpublished doctoral dissertation). The George Washington University, Washington, DC.

Confessore, G. J. (1992). An introduction to the study of self-directed learning. In G. J. Confessore & S. J. Confessore (Eds.), *Guideposts to self-directed learning: Expert commentary on essential concepts* (pp. 1-6). King of Prussia, PA: Organization Design and Development.

Confessore, G. J., & Park, E. (2004). Factor validation of the Learner Autonomy Profile, version 3.0 and extraction of the short form. *International Journal of Self-directed Learning, 1*(1), 39-58.

Cureton, E. E., & D'Agostino, R. B. (1983). *Factor analysis: An applied approach.* Hillsdale, NJ: Lawrence Erlbaum Associates.

Derrick, M. G. (2001). *The measurement of an adult's intention to exhibit persistence in autonomous learning* (Unpublished doctoral dissertation). The George Washington University, Washington, DC.

Dunteman, G. H. (1989). *Principal components analysis.* Newbury Park, CA: SAGE.

Fishbein, M., & Ajzen, I. (1975). *Belief, attitude, intention, and behavior: An introduction to theory and research.* Reading, MA: Addison-Wesley.

Gorsuch, R. L. (1983). *Factor analysis.* Hillsdale, NJ: Lawrence Erlbaum Associates.

Hinkle, D. E., Wiersma, W., & Jurs, S. G. (1998). *Applied statistics for the behavioral sciences* (4th ed.). Boston, MA: Houghton Mifflin.

Kim, J., & Mueller, C. W. (1978). *Introduction to factor analysis: What it is and how to do it.* Beverly Hills, CA: SAGE.

Kline, P. (1993). *The handbook of psychological testing.* New York, NY: Routledge.

Meyer, D. T. (2001). *The measurement of intentional behavior as a prerequisite to autonomous learning* (Unpublished doctoral dissertation). The George Washington University, Washington, DC.

Norusis, M. J. (1988). *SPSS-X advanced statistics guide* (2nd ed.). Chicago, IL: SPSS.

Ponton, M. K. (1999). *The measurement of an adult's intention to exhibit personal initiative in autonomous learning* (Unpublished doctoral dissertation). The George Washington University, Washington, DC.

Ponton, M. K., & Carr, P. B. (2000). Understanding and promoting autonomy in self-directed learning. *Current Research in Social Psychology, 5*(19). Retrieved from http://www.uiowa.edu/crisp/ **[cf. Chapter 2]**

Ponton, M. K., Carr, P. B., & Derrick, M. G. (2003, February). *A path analysis of the conative factors associated with autonomous learning.* Paper presented at the 17th International Self-Directed Learning Symposium, Cocoa Beach, FL. **[cf. Chapter 8]**

Ponton, M. K., Derrick, M. G., Carr, P. B., & Hall, J. M. (2004). *The relationship between self-efficacy and autonomous learning.* Paper presented at the 18th International Self-Directed Learning Symposium, Cocoa Beach, FL. **[cf. Chapter 12]**

CHAPTER 11

SELF-EFFICACY TO DO OR SELF-EFFICACY TO LEARN TO DO: A STUDY RELATED TO PERSEVERANCE[11]

Bandura (1995) asserted that "efficacy beliefs play a vital role in the development of self-directed lifelong learners" (p. 17). This descriptive study sought to determine if perseverance in performances without a history of success are more likely due to beliefs of self-efficacy in the performance itself or to beliefs of self-efficacy to learn the performance. This is a conceptual nuance not previously investigated in self-efficacy research. Findings suggest that self-efficacy to learn is as important as self-efficacy to do with respect to perseverant behavior in unmastered activities despite repeated failures.

The enactment of novel pursuits is a common characteristic of human agency (i.e., intentional action). Both the advancement of a technological society as well as the creation of a self-fulfilling life depend upon self-selecting new courses of action that build upon previously acquired knowledge and skills. Due to the novelty of such pursuits, learning is a requisite component in achieving mastery and ultimate success. In addition, the self-selecting aspect of novel pursuits often requires the agent (i.e., the person exhibiting agency) to engage in self-directed learning where *"self-directed* learning represents the degree to which personal agency is exercised individually by directing the creation of . . . [learning] activities" (Ponton, 2009, p. 65).

According to social cognitive theory, the most central percept in defining and shaping human agency is self-efficacy (Bandura, 1986). Courses of action are chosen and persevered in dependent upon self-appraisals of personal capability to muster strategies perceived as necessary for success (Bandura, 1997). When engaging in a novel pursuit, self-efficacy appraisals may include not only the ability to engage in the activity itself (i.e., "self-efficacy to do"; presently labeled

[11]This article is reprinted with permission from the *International Journal for Self-Directed Learning* (http://sdlglobal.com/journals.php) and is copyrighted © The International Society for Self-Directed Learning [2014, *11*(1), 29-40]

performing self-efficacy) but also the ability to learn how to engage in the activity (i.e., "self-efficacy to learn to do"; presently labeled *learning self-efficacy*). The purpose of this chapter is to differentiate the import of these two appraisals as they relate to perseverant behavior in unmastered activities despite failed attempts.

Theoretical Framework

Bandura (2001) asserted the following:

> Efficacy beliefs are the foundation of human agency. Unless people believe they can produce desired results and forestall detrimental ones by their actions, they have little incentive to act or to *persevere* [emphasis added] in the face of difficulties. Whatever other factors may operate as guides and motivators, they are rooted in the core belief that one has the power to produce effects by one's actions. (p. 10)

Self-efficacy refers to a personal belief that one has the capability "to organize and execute the courses of action required to produce given attainments" (Bandura, 1997, p. 3). In this regard, self-efficacy is not a mere inventory of existing knowledge and skills but rather is "perceived operative capability" (Bandura, 2007, p. 646); that is, self-efficacy is based upon a personal appraisal of what one is able to do with whatever resources one can make available. As a belief, self-efficacy is not a simple reflection of objective assessments that measure skills of organization and execution but rather is developed through personal interpretations of efficacy information; thus, self-efficacy is a self-perception and must be measured as such.

In general, humans do not choose to engage in activities that they perceive as ineffectual in producing desirable outcomes; thus, much of human activity is cognitively motivated due to our capability of forethought but mediated by personal appraisals of efficacy (Bandura, 1986, 1997). Social cognitive theory recognizes three categories of outcomes—social (e.g., money, praise, ostracism), personal (e.g., pleasure, pain), and self-evaluative (i.e., congruence to personal standards)—that represent consequences to performances (Bandura, 1997). Agents choose activities and adopt performance goals based not only upon the perceived relationship to obtaining desirable outcomes or avoiding aversive ones but also upon whether or not perceived capability exists to muster a successful performance (Bandura, 1997).

Self-efficacy has been an explicit part of the self-directed learning literature for approximately 20 years (cf. Bloyd, Hoban, & Wall, 1995; Hoban & Hoban, 2004; Ponton, Carr, Schuette, & Confessore, 2010; Ponton, Derrick, Confessore, & Rhea, 2005; Ponton, Derrick, Hall, Rhea, & Carr, 2005; Wall, Sersland, & Hoban, 1996). Hoban and Hoban (2004) stated the following: "The work of so many of those who have applied the concept of self-efficacy to learning confirms Bandura's postulation of the link between self-efficacy and self-directed learning. That seems undeniably clear" (p. 21). More recent empiricism (Ponton, Carr, et al., 2010) and theorizing (Ponton, 2009) continue to support the assertion that "efficacy beliefs play a vital role in the development of self-directed lifelong learners" (Bandura, 1995, p. 17). Quite simply, an individual will not choose to engage in a self-directed learning activity or, subsequently, persevere in one in the face of failed attempts unless that person believes that he or she possesses the capability to successfully execute such a learning activity.

There are four primary sources of efficacy information: mastery experiences, verbal persuasion, vicarious experiences, and physiological/emotive arousals (Bandura, 1977). In general, mastery experiences foster percepts of efficacy when successful performances are attributed to personal capability. In addition, verbal assurances of capability provided by credible others can strengthen efficacy. Observing the modeled capabilities of similar others provides a vicarious mechanism that may also increase one's belief in personal abilities. Finally, interpretations of somatic feedback resulting from a performance may strengthen efficacy if such arousals are interpreted as epiphenomenal to the activity and a natural accompaniment to expanding capability. However, regardless of the source of information,

> it is the agent and not some external evaluator who
> reflects upon the varied forms of efficacy information
> and arrives at a resultant efficacy belief – self-efficacy
> is perceived capability developed subjectively through
> one's cognitive filters, not some objectified assessment
> of capability. (Ponton, 2009, p. 72)

Note that "self-efficacy is a domain specific assessment" (Ponton, Derrick, Confessore, & Rhea, 2005, p. 86); that is, personal capabilities are appraised to varying degrees based upon each separate activity under scrutiny. For example, it is an entirely different efficacy appraisal regarding one's ability to drive a car versus one's ability to learn how to drive a car. For unmastered activities and in the face of failed attempts, there would seemingly be authentic indicators of a lack of capability that logically might weaken performing efficacy (i.e., self-efficacy to do); therefore, perseverance would suggest a strong sense of learning efficacy (i.e., self-efficacy to learn to do). Thus, *it is hypothesized that perseverant behavior is highly dependent upon an agent's belief in his or her ability to learn to perform the unmastered pursuit.* In order to fully understand perseverant behavior, domain-correct appraisals of efficacy must be studied.

Procedures

Instrumentation

The Appraisal of Differential Efficacy (ADE; see Appendix) was developed to assess the comparative importance of performing self-efficacy (i.e., self-efficacy to do) versus learning self-efficacy (i.e., self-efficacy to learn to do) with respect to perseverant behavior in an unmastered activity and in the face of failed attempts. "Efficacy beliefs should be measured in terms of particularized judgments of capability that may vary . . . under different situational circumstances" (Bandura, 1997, p. 42); thus, the construction of the four efficacy items adhered to a format of providing a situation with varying sources of efficacy information followed by fixed response choices designed to uncover the comparative importance of both forms of efficacy. Each of the four efficacy items attended to the four sources of efficacy information as follows:

- Item 1 focused solely on the lack of a mastery experience;
- Despite the lack of a mastery experience, Item 2 included the provision of a positive verbal persuasion;
- Despite the lack of a mastery experience, Item 3 included the provision of a positive vicarious experience; and
- With the lack of a mastery experience, Item 4 included the provision of a negative physiological or emotive arousal.

As this is an exploratory study, a simple instrument was desired to provide some indication as to the differential import of both percepts of self-efficacy—performing versus learning—not only when there is no information to strengthen performing self-efficacy beliefs (i.e., Items 1 and 4) but also when there is such information (i.e., Items 2 and 3); however, in all items the most authentic indicator of performing self-efficacy—a mastery experience—is lacking in the initiation of the activity ("engaged in an activity in which you have never performed successfully in the past") and in its continued enactment ("persist in overcoming failed attempts").

"The item content of self-efficacy scales must represent beliefs about personal abilities to produce specified levels of performance" (Bandura, 1997, p. 45); thus, the fixed response choices explicitly attend to these guidelines and support construct validity by incorporating measures of belief ("I believe"), personal ability ("I am able to"), and specific level of performance ("perform the activity successfully"). In addition, "to achieve explanatory and predictive power, measures of personal efficacy must be tailored to domains of functioning"; construct validity is again supported by the phrases "able to perform" and "able to learn how to perform" that differentiate performing and learning efficacy, respectively. Note that self-efficacy scales rely on construct validation to a great degree (Bandura, 1997). The participant is asked to select the self-efficacy appraisal that "best describes" perseverant behavior in order to provide an indication as to the differential import of both percepts of self-efficacy. It is purported that the ADE is face valid in that the measure associated with each item is consistent with its construction and underlying theoretical framework.

The Flesch-Kincaid Grade Level of the ADE is 6.1 (as per Microsoft Word 2013 analysis). The first author administered the ADE to all participants completing the paper version; none of these 46 participants expressed any confusion with respect to understanding any aspect of the instrument.

Sample

The population of interest was adults (i.e., minimum age of 18 years). Because a random sample of this population could not be targeted and accessed, data from various samples of convenience were collected (N = 102) in order to perform the study (cf. Gall, Gall, & Borg's, 2007, p. 175, justification for convenience sampling). The participants were targeted to produce variation in age and education as these characteristics likely provide efficacy information in the two domains of interest (i.e., performing and learning) due to associated experiences. The majority were female (n = 69; P = 67.6%) and the levels of education were as follows: high school diploma/G.E.D., n = 48, P = 47.1%; bachelor's degree, n = 12, P = 11.8%; and graduate/professional degree, n = 42, P = 41.2%. The largest age range represented by the sample was 18-22 (n = 48; P = 47.1%; see Table 1). Note that 46 participants completed the paper version of the ADE (see Appendix) that allowed for the submission of age in years, whereas 56 participants completed an online version of the ADE that provided age ranges corresponding to Table 1; thus, the 46 exact ages submitted were converted to the age ranges presented.

Table 1. Age Ranges of Participants

Age Range	n	P
18-22	48	47.1
23-27	7	6.8
28-32	7	6.8
33-37	8	7.8
38-42	11	10.8
43-47	5	4.9
48-52	6	5.9
53-57	5	4.9
58-62	3	2.9
63-67	1	1.0
68-72	0	0.0
73-77	1	1.0

Findings

Tables 2 through 5 present the findings associated with ADE Items 1 through 4, respectively. Margins of error assume large populations (Creative Research Systems, 2012). Statistically significant differences in percentages relative to performing efficacy (i.e., Response a) were calculated (Vassar College, n.d.).

For all four items, participants indicated that perseverance is based upon equal strengths of performing and learning self-efficacy to a greater degree than merely performing self-efficacy; for three items (Item 2 excluded; see Table 3), participants indicated that perseverance is based upon learning self-efficacy to a greater degree than merely performing self-efficacy. Thus, the research hypothesis that learning self-efficacy is as important in perseverant behavior as performing self-efficacy is supported; for three items, learning self-efficacy is more important than performing self-efficacy.

Table 2. Item 1 - Lack of Mastery Experience

Response Option	n	P	Margin of Error[a]
a. I believe I am able to perform the activity successfully	11	10.8	6.0
b. I believe I am able to learn how to perform the activity successfully	46	45.1[b]	9.7
c. I believe a and b equally	44	43.1[b]	9.6
d. I do not believe a or b	1	1.0	1.9

[a]For CI_{95} assuming a large population. [b]Different from Response a at the nondirectional .0001 level.

Table 3. Item 2 - Lack of Mastery Experience With Positive Verbal Persuasion

Response Option	n	P	Margin of Error[a]
a. I believe I am able to perform the activity successfully	19	18.6	7.6
b. I believe I am able to learn how to perform the activity successfully	32	31.4	9.0
c. I believe a and b equally	51	50.0[b,c]	9.7
d. I do not believe a or b	0	0.0	n/a

[a]For CI_{95} assuming a large population. [b]Different from Response a at the nondirectional .0001 level. [c]Different from Response b at the nondirectional .05 level.

Table 4. Item 3 - Lack of Mastery Experience With Positive Vicarious Experience

Response Option	n	P	Margin of Error[a]
a. I believe I am able to perform the activity successfully	19	18.6	7.6
b. I believe I am able to learn how to perform the activity successfully	36	35.3[b]	9.3
c. I believe a and b equally	46	45.1[c]	9.7
d. I do not believe a or b	1	1.0	1.9

[a]For CI_{95} assuming a large population. [b]Different from Response a at the nondirectional .025 level. [c]Different from Response a at the nondirectional .0005 level.

Table 5. Item 4 - Lack of Mastery Experience With Negative Physiological or Emotive Arousal

Response Option	n	P	Margin of Error[a]
a. I believe I am able to perform the activity successfully	11	10.8	6.0
b. I believe I am able to learn how to perform the activity successfully	44	43.1[b]	9.6
c. I believe a and b equally	37	36.3[b]	9.3
d. I do not believe a or b	10	9.8	5.8

[a]For CI_{95} assuming a large population. [b]Different from Response a at the nondirectional .0001 level.

Discussion

The major threat to internal validity was the use of new instrumentation; however, the internal consistency of the findings for the four separate efficacy situations presented provides evidence that the interpretation of the results is consistent with the instrument's proposed purpose to measure differential efficacy (cf. Creswell, 2015, p. 158, regarding instrument validity). The major threat to external validity was the nonprobability sample of adults measured; thus, the following conclusions, implications, and recommendations may not be generalizable to the entire adult population.

The present findings suggest that perseverance in unmastered activities despite failed attempts is heavily dependent upon the agent's learning self-efficacy rather than merely performing self-efficacy. This is true even in the presence of information (via verbal persuasion and vicarious experiences) that may enhance performing efficacy. The implication of this finding is that we, as educators, must move toward developing people who believe strongly in their ability to learn challenging, novel content.

It is not enough to expect that learning successes demonstrated by objective assessments will be reflected as stronger efficacy beliefs for learning; this is an overly simplistic view of enactive mastery experiences (cf. Bandura, 1997). Self-efficacy is a self-perception and, as such, is influenced by cognitive processes developed through reflections of varied sources of efficacy information amassed over time; thus, preexisting percepts of efficacy influence how new efficacy information is processed. Learning successes may raise, not change, or even diminish percepts of self-efficacy depending upon how the person interprets this new information through existing cognitive biases (Bandura, 1997).

By exerting too much control, an educator may reduce the potential for learning experiences to strengthen students' learning efficacy. In order to promote a student's self-efficacy to learn, the educator must understand to what degree complex learning activities need to be simplified in order to provide sufficient challenges that strengthen percepts of coping strategies related to learning. The educator must decide what constitutes a "sufficient" challenge based upon an understanding of the student's capabilities and similar others at the same developmental stage. Mastery experiences that strengthen learning efficacy should be difficult but accomplishable tasks that require (a) the use of extant cognitive and metacognitive strategies in novel activities to overcome learning challenges, (b) personal goal setting coupled with assessments that highlight incremental growth and expanding development of individual knowledge and skills, and (c) self-reliance that provides an opportunity for the student to attribute learning successes to personal efficacy rather than nonability factors such as a good teacher or excellent resources.

Coupled with enactive mastery experiences, educators should provide persuading feedback that validates to the student his or her ability to learn new knowledge and acquire new skills. Typically armed with assessed indicators of growth, educators are in a good position to convey to students that personal capabilities to learn novel, challenging content are expanding. Armed with similar information from mastery experiences, students are in a good position to evaluate the accuracy of such feedback and, thus, the credibility of the persuaders thereby affecting the ability of these persuaders to strengthen students' learning efficacy via expressed appraisals. In general, learning efficacy is enhanced when learning successes are associated with expanding capabilities rather than dint of effort; in fact, to convey that success is greatly related to hard work suggests effort is required to offset a lack of ability thereby possibly weakening efficacy appraisals (Bandura, 1997). Therefore, educators should provide persuasive feedback grounded in accurate diagnoses of accomplishment and couched in terms of a student's expanding capability to learn in order to strengthen learning self-efficacy. To spawn continued growth by tackling even greater learning challenges such as those likely represented by novel pursuits, persuaders should also provide efficacy appraisals in moderate excess of current capabilities to facilitate greater attainments "through better strategy selection and extra effort . . . [without a great risk of failure that may] undermine the diagnostic credibility of the persuaders and further reinforce performers' belief in their inherent limitations" (Bandura, 1997, p. 105). Human achievement and increased capability are rooted in successful endeavors that stretch current capacities; such endeavors are typically chosen when personal appraisals of capability exceed actual capability—at least to some degree—whereby the latter is then enhanced due to the accomplished performance.

People often appraise their capabilities based upon social comparisons particularly when little if any direct experiences are present; thus, efficacy is appraised via vicarious experiences in which the competency of similar others is observed, assessed, and projected onto the observer (Bandura, 1997). Educators should identify models who are as similar as possible to current students but possess greater capabilities and then create learning activities that allow the students to observe the models' successful strategies. The assessment of similarity should be based upon attributes (e.g., similar in appearance) as well as ability (e.g., similar or slightly more talented; avoid high-achieving models who have talents that far exceed observers thus creating humbling social comparisons that may weaken an observer's efficacy). Models should fulfill an instructional role so that observers can develop skills and strengthen percepts of efficacy in manageable pursuits facilitated by identifying with the model and then observing the model's capabilities, expressed thought patterns, and associated achievements. Models should be chosen not based solely upon similarities but also with respect to being encouragers of success; chosen in this manner, models will support not only attentional, retentional, and production processes necessary for observational learning to occur but also requisite motivational processes via verbal encouragement (cf. Bandura, 1986). In our current technological age, models do not have to be physically present. Models can interact with observers symbolically via visual media as they "convey rules for generative and innovative behavior . . . [by verbalizing] their thought processes and strategies aloud as they engage in problem-solving activities" (Bandura, 1997, p. 93); thus, adequate models may be incorporated into instruction with few geographic limitations.

Physiological and emotive arousals resulting from performances also represent a source of efficacy information. Like the other three sources discussed, the effect of this information on percepts of efficacy is not direct; it is mediated by cognitive processing. Educators can help students to use this information in efficacy building ways by influencing how somatic feedback is interpreted. Sociocognitive theory suggests that "knowledge about bodily states is acquired, in large part, through social labeling coordinated with experienced events" (Bandura, 1997, p. 107; cf. Bandura, 1986); thus, educators can play a role in this labeling process. Whether it is feedback associated with strength from a physical activity (e.g., body aches, fatigue) or associated with discomfort from an emotionally tense situation (e.g., elevated pulse rate, sweating), such arousals are likely to occur even though they may be unobservable. Thus, educators should recognize the likelihood of such feedback and proactively work toward helping students to interpret such reactions as just the natural course of events when new knowledge or skills are being developed. Educators should also be careful not to create activities that are so daunting as to elicit extreme somatic reactions thereby diminishing the opportunity for both success and the strengthening of efficacy. The educator must decide an appropriate level of challenge based upon an understanding of the student's capabilities as well as observed somatic feedback. In addition, educators can help students to focus on the activity at hand instead of physiological or emotive arousals. Consequently, students can increase the probability of a successful performance through increased attention on the performance itself thereby facilitating increases in capability and stronger percepts of efficacy. By proactively fostering efficacy promoting interpretations of somatic arousals, learning facilitators could greatly reduce the need for cognitive reframing (i.e., changing how students currently interpret such arousals).

Concluding Remarks

If the motivation to pursue a novel activity were solely dependent upon an agent's self-efficacy to perform the activity itself, then it would be up to the agent to strengthen self-perceptions of ability using extant sources of efficacy information. The findings of the present study suggest that in comparison to self-efficacy with respect to the performance, self-efficacy to learn the performance is equally important, if not more important, to motivate perseverant behavior in the face of failed attempts. One's efficacy beliefs about learning provide a measure of control within challenging contexts (i.e., novel pursuits) that often include failed attempts on the path to mastery. Persons efficacious in learning are better able to cope with failed attempts by perceiving each failure as a means to diagnose weaknesses, reevaluate and revise action plans, and try again. For example, an athlete who perseveringly seeks out improvement using coaches, models, and personally acquired information does so with the belief that he or she has the ability to learn how to perform in the chosen sport.

This finding represents a great opportunity for educators to influence the human pursuit of unmastered activities by strengthening students' learning efficacy. Educators should attend to the four sources of efficacy information in constructing learning activities that facilitate learning and build a strong sense of efficacy to learn challenging content. Such efficacy will empower students to pursue novel activities that promote higher levels of personal development and satisfaction. In addition, theorists should also consider these findings as they suggest a necessity to incorporate both performing and learning efficacy instruments in research in order to maximize the explanatory and predictive power of measured constructs used to understand human performance.

Initiatives at the institutional level should also be developed to promote the strengthening of students' efficacy to learn. Developmental programs can help educators—professional teachers/administrators or nonprofessionals such as teaching assistants and student peers—to understand the theory of the proposed efficacy building activities and their instructional applications; note that educators must also possess a strong sense of efficacy to engage in this type of instruction in order to maximize their motivation and effectiveness in doing so. In particular, peer-assisted learning (e.g., supplemental instruction, peer tutoring) should be designed to take full advantage of the opportunity for vicarious experiences to strengthen students' percepts of efficacy via social modeling. All these initiatives will help to foster an institutional culture that supports and encourages efficacy building transactions between educators and students.

People exert considerable influence over the courses that their lives take. Their personal values, interests, and appraisals of capability are informed by experiences and interactions with environmental circumstances. Drawing upon these informational resources, they individually decide novel pursuits that cause considerable divergences between individual life trajectories. It is not uncommon to experience failures in performing novel pursuits as they can challenge existing competencies thereby requiring additional knowledge or skills. Previous theoretical arguments have suggested that perseverance in the face of failed attempts is dependent upon a strong sense of efficacy in the performance itself; however, the present study suggests an equal, if not more important, dependence upon a strong sense of efficacy to learn the performance. Because novel pursuits may require novel learning activities, perseverance in self-chosen pursuits may be strongly dependent upon an agent's efficacy to engage in self-directed learning. Further research is needed to provide support for this assertion.

References

Bandura, A. (1977). Self-efficacy: Toward a unifying theory of behavioral change. *Psychological Review, 84*(2), 191-215.

Bandura, A. (1986). *Social foundations of thought and action: A social cognitive theory.* Englewood Cliffs, NJ: Prentice Hall.

Bandura, A. (1995). Exercise of personal and collective efficacy in changing societies. In A. Bandura (Ed.), *Self-efficacy in changing societies* (pp. 1-45). Cambridge, UK: Cambridge University Press.

Bandura, A. (1997). *Self-efficacy: The exercise of control.* New York, NY: W. H. Freeman and Company.

Bandura, A. (2001). Social cognitive theory: An agentic perspective. *Annual Review of Psychology, 52*, 1-26.

Bandura, A. (2007). Much ado over a faulty conception of perceived self-efficacy grounded in faulty experimentation. *Journal of Social and Clinical Psychology, 26*(6), 641-658.

Bloyd, R., Hoban, G., & Wall, A. D. (1995). Self-efficacy and the adult learner: Implications for the teaching of writing. In H. B. Long & Associates (Eds.), *New dimensions in self-directed learning* (pp. 197-215). Norman, OK: Public Managers Center, University of Oklahoma.

Creative Research Systems. (2012). *Sample size calculator.* Retrieved from http://www .surveysystem.com/sscalc.htm

Creswell, J. W. (2015). *Educational research: Planning, conducting, and evaluating quantitative and qualitative research* (5th ed.). Upper Saddle River, NJ: Pearson Education.

Gall, M. D., Gall, J. P., & Borg, W. R. (2007). *Educational research: An introduction* (8th ed.). Boston, MA: Pearson Education.

Hoban, S., & Hoban, G. (2004). Self-esteem, self-efficacy and self-directed learning: Attempting to undo the confusion. *International Journal of Self-Directed Learning, 2*(1), 7-25.

Ponton, M. K. (2009). An agentic perspective contrasting autonomous learning with self-directed learning. In M. G. Derrick & M. K. Ponton (Eds.), *Emerging directions in self-directed learning* (pp. 65-76). Chicago, IL: Discovery Association Publishing House. **[cf. Chapter 4]**

Ponton, M. K., Carr, P. B., Schuette, C. T., & Confessore, G. J. (2010). Self-efficacy and the Learner Autonomy Profile. *International Journal of Self-Directed Learning, 7*(2), 54-63. **[cf. Chapter 14]**

Ponton, M. K., Derrick, M. G., Confessore, G. J., & Rhea, N. (2005). The role of self-efficacy in autonomous learning. *International Journal of Self-directed Learning, 2*(2), 81-90. **[cf. Chapter 10]**

Ponton, M. K., Derrick, M. G., Hall, J. M., Rhea, N. E., & Carr, P. B. (2005). The relationship between self-efficacy and autonomous learning: The development of new instrumentation. *International Journal of Self-Directed Learning, 2*(1), 50-61. **[cf. Chapter 12]**

Vassar College. (n.d.). *Calculators.* Retrieved from http://faculty.vassar.edu/lowry/polls /calcs.html

Wall, A. D., Sersland, C. J., & Hoban, G. (1996). The adult learner's self-efficacy, readiness for self-directed learning, and gender: Implication for math performance. In H. B. Long & Associates (Eds.), *Current developments in self-directed learning* (pp. 107-125). Norman, OK: Public Managers Center, University of Oklahoma.

APPENDIX

Appraisal of Differential Efficacy – Paper Version

For items 1 through 4, please circle the letter of the response that best describes you:

1. When engaged in an activity in which you have never performed successfully in the past, which of the following best describes why you persist in overcoming failed attempts:

   a. I believe I am able to perform the activity successfully.
   b. I believe I am able to learn how to perform the activity successfully.
   c. I believe a and b equally.
   d. I do not believe a or b.

2. When engaged in an activity in which you have never performed successfully in the past but that someone whose opinion you value tells you that you can perform the activity successfully, which of the following best describes why you persist in overcoming failed attempts:

   a. I believe I am able to perform the activity successfully.
   b. I believe I am able to learn how to perform the activity successfully.
   c. I believe a and b equally.
   d. I do not believe a or b.

3. When engaged in an activity in which you have never performed successfully in the past but that you notice that someone who is very much like you can perform the activity successfully, which of the following best describes why you persist in overcoming failed attempts:

   a. I believe I am able to perform the activity successfully.
   b. I believe I am able to learn how to perform the activity successfully.
   c. I believe a and b equally.
   d. I do not believe a or b.

4. When engaged in an activity in which you have never performed successfully in the past and that causes you either physical or emotional discomfort when engaged in the activity, which of the following best describes why you persist in overcoming failed attempts:

   a. I believe I am able to perform the activity successfully.
   b. I believe I am able to learn how to perform the activity successfully.
   c. I believe a and b equally.
   d. I do not believe a or b.

Please provide the following information:

a. Gender (circle one):   Male   Female

b. Age in years (enter number): _____

c. What is the highest diploma or degree you have earned (circle one)?

   High school diploma or GED

   Bachelor's degree

   Graduate degree

CHAPTER 12

THE RELATIONSHIP BETWEEN SELF-EFFICACY AND AUTONOMOUS LEARNING: THE DEVELOPMENT OF NEW INSTRUMENTATION[12]

Previous work has shown that cognized goals and outcome expectancies motivate engagement in specific behaviors through the mediating influence of self-efficacy. Autonomous learning represents a specific set of behaviors as measured by intentions to show resourcefulness, initiative, and persistence in one's learning; thus, self-efficacy in autonomous learning should precede a learner's participation in autonomous learning activities. The purpose of the present study was to develop a self-efficacy in autonomous learning instrument thereby enabling future research to test this hypothesized causal relationship. Two pilot studies were conducted in this developmental process: the first pilot study (N = 77) focused on instrument parsimony while the second study (N = 51) was conducted to confirm item homogeneity and internal consistency of the resultant instrument. The results suggest that the final form of the Appraisal of Learner Autonomy is both valid and reliable thereby enabling future research into this psychological factor associated with learner autonomy.

In 1992, Confessore asserted that in order for self-directed learning to lead to a personally satisfying conclusion, the factors of desire, resourcefulness, initiative, and persistence must be manifest. Over the past 5 years, researchers have developed valid instrumentation to assess these factors (Carr, 1999; Derrick, 2001; Meyer, 2001; Ponton, 1999), with continuing levels of refinement (cf. Park & Confessore, 2002), in an attempt to supply the field of self-directed learning with new research based insights into these aspects of autonomous learning.

---

[12]This article is reprinted with permission from the *International Journal for Self-Directed Learning* (http://sdlglobal.com/journals.php) and is copyrighted © The International Society for Self-Directed Learning [2005, *2*(1), 50-61]

Ponton (1999) defined learner autonomy as "the characteristic of the person who independently exhibits agency [i.e., intentional behavior] in learning activities" (pp. 13-14) and stated that autonomy represents a subset of the attributes (i.e., agentic actions) associated with self-directedness. Ponton suggested that autonomy, like self-directedness, represent cognitive and affective qualities of the agent while autonomous learning refers to subsequent conative manifestations. The term "conative" is used with aspects of autonomous learning because "conation refers to his [sic, i.e., the agent's] behavioral intentions" (Fishbein &Ajzen, 1975, p. 12) and ensuing intentional activity.

A recent path-analytic study conducted by Ponton, Carr, and Derrick (2003), however, concluded that a measure of self-efficacy in autonomous learning was needed "to better describe the relationship between motivation and conation" (p. 13). This recommendation was based upon the lack of context with respect to adult autonomous learning associated with Meyer's (2001) desire measure and the important role of self-efficacy as a predictor of human performance (Bandura & Locke, 2003). Meyer created the Inventory of Learner Desire (ILD) as an assessment of the degree to which an agent can act intentionally, independent of any particular contextual manifestation; thus, its explanatory utility within the context of autonomous learning was questioned (Ponton, Carr, & Derrick, 2003). Contrary to the ILD, the Inventory of Learner Resourcefulness (ILR; Carr, 1999), the Inventory of Learner Initiative (ILI; Ponton, 1999), and the Inventory of Learner Persistence (ILP; Derrick, 2001) were constructed to assess intentions of respective subscales within the domain of adult learning.

Hoban and Sersland (1998) performed a study to determine if a correlation existed between readiness for self-directed learning (assessed via the Self-Directed Learning Readiness Survey) and self-efficacy for self-directed learning. As part of this investigation, the 10-item Self-Efficacy for Self-Directed Learning Questionnaire (SSLQ) was developed. A statistically significant correlation was found ($r = 0.49$, $N = 86$, $p < .001$) between the two measures for a sample of students who were tested at the beginning of their teacher credentialing program. This research suggested that self-efficacy is an important construct in understanding a student's readiness for self-directed learning.

For the purposes of investigations on the larger population of adult learners, however, the SSLQ is inadequate due to items that are expressly related to structured education. References to "teacher" (item

2, Hoban & Sersland, 1998, p. 17), "fellow students" (item 4, p. 17), "student directed cooperative groups" (item 6, p. 17), "instructional videotapes" (item 8, p. 18), and "graduate courses" (item 10, p. 18) suggest that the SSLQ's validity is related to its use on adults participating in formal graduate education. However, the concept of autonomous learning as an agentic activity is not limited to students participating in educational programs. While such students certainly can exhibit autonomy in their learning, other adults may do so as well. Thus, a new instrument was required to measure self-efficacy within the construct of autonomous learning.

The purpose of the present study was to develop an instrument to measure self-efficacy in autonomous learning. Such an instrument would use the guidelines presented by Bandura (2001) in developing self-efficacy scales, and testing would be performed to support validity and reliability. The hypothesized role of self-efficacy with autonomous learning will be presented along with results from the instrument development activity.

Theoretical Framework

Fishbein and Ajzen (1975) provided a simple model relating beliefs, attitudes, intentions, and behaviors. They described beliefs as a cognitive process in which objects are assigned attributes that provide a discrimination function; that is, cognition is one's knowledge. Attitudes are a learned affection of favor or disfavor with respect to different objects based upon the discriminating attributes where such attitudes may influence (in addition to being influenced by) beliefs. Attitudes toward objects then influence the intentions of the agent and subsequent behaviors where the consequences of behaviors provide feedback to one's belief system. This model is presented in Chapter 1, Figure 1.

Based upon past research, Bandura (1997) summarized the mediating influence of self-efficacy on cognitive motivation. An agent will not engage in performances and adopt performance goals that are thought to lead to desirable outcomes unless the agent feels efficacious in effecting a successful performance (cf. Ponton, Edmister, Ukeiley, & Seiner, 2001). People do not engage in perceived futile endeavors but rather choose activities that they feel will lead to satisfying ends. Through self-reflection, people process different sources of efficacy information (i.e., mastery experiences, vicarious experiences, verbal persuasion, and physiological/emotive arousals) and form beliefs about their level of capability in diverse arenas. Using this knowledge, favorable or unfavorable attitudes toward engagement in select behaviors are developed that influence activity choice. Thus, self-efficacy precedes conation.

Self-efficacy is a domain specific assessment. One's perception of capability in turning on a light switch is typically much different than an assessment of capability in running a 4-minute mile. Therefore, assessments of efficacy must be contextualized to the activity of interest. The context of autonomous learning is no different. If one believes that engagement in autonomous learning activities will lead to desirable outcomes and feels capable of successfully doing such learning, then it should be expected that self-efficacy in autonomous learning should precede such learning.

As previously mentioned Meyer's (2001) instrument of desire is not contextualized to adult autonomous learning but rather is an assessment of an adult's ability to exert influence over his or her life by considering the three subscales of freedom, power, and change. Her instrument represents "an attempt to measure the degree to which an agent can act intentionally" (Ponton, Carr, & Derrick, 2003, p. 2) or as Park and Confessore (2002) asserted, "[Meyer's] work on desire to learn has been treated as an effort to understand the *precursors* to the development of intentions related to learning" (p. 289). Unfortunately, without a behavioral context, one's general belief concerning the ability to act intentionally will probably provide little explanatory utility in understanding specific conative manifestations such as autonomous learning. If autonomous learning is determined by a summation of the ILR, ILI, and ILP and using the presented arguments of context, it is hypothesized that the largest effect on autonomous learning will be through the path

Desire $\longrightarrow$ *Self-Efficacy in Autonomous Learning* $\longrightarrow$ *Autonomous Learning*

where self-efficacy should mediate the influence of desire on autonomous learning. Because of the past lack of suitable self-efficacy instrumentation, research on testing the hypothesized path analytic model represents future work.

Development of the Appraisal of Learner Autonomy

First Pilot Study

The Appraisal of Learner Autonomy (ALA; Appendix A) was constructed using the ideas presented by Bandura (2001) and modeled after the Exercise Self-Efficacy Scale (ESS; Bandura, 2001, p. 11) by permission (Bandura, personal communication, October 6, 2003). As per Bandura's (2001) guidelines, the title of the ALA does not include "self-efficacy" to avoid response bias (Bandura, p. 6), the scale is in gradations of "can do" to reflect a measure of capability (Bandura, p. 4), the scale ranges from 0-100 to improve predictive utility (Pajares, Hartley, & Valiante, 2001), the text is domain specific to autonomous learning to improve both predictive and explanatory utility within this construct (Bandura, p. 1), and the items represent performance impediments to maximize discrimination between respondents (Bandura, p. 3).

The introductory statement in the ALA (see Appendix A) reads as follows:

> Please rate how sure you are that you can get yourself to participate in a learning activity when nobody else requires you to do so. Note that a learning activity is any activity that you believe will help you to learn something that you want to learn.

This statement reflects the position of Ponton, Carr, and Confessore (2000) that autonomous learning is an agentic activity where agency refers to behavior that is intentional and based upon a multitude of sociocognitive determinants. Self-efficacy is asserted to be relevant to autonomous learning as manifest agency because "perceived self-efficacy is an important part of that constellation of unmeasured determinants of performance" (Bandura & Locke, 2003, p. 91).

Social cognitive theory posits the existence of three types of barriers to agency: cognitive (i.e., self-inefficacy), situational (i.e., temporary), and structural (i.e., inadequate resources; Bandura, 1997); however, in general, the items presented in the ESS scale include situational impediments applicable to any type of adult activity. The original 21-item version of the ALA (Appendix A) included 20 items directly associated with the complete ESS that were either (a) taken verbatim (ALA items 1-3, 7, 8, 11-15, 19, and 21), (b) contextualized to learning as opposed to exercise (ALA items 4, 9, and 10), (c) separated to avoid double-barreled items (ALA items 5, 6, 17, 18), or (d) rewritten slightly (ALA item 16). Only ALA item 20 is new and reflects a structural barrier (i.e., monetary cost) as suggested by Darkenwald and Valentine (1985) as a deterrent to adult learning.

Bandura (2001) argued that self-efficacy scales are face valid; however, research directed at establishing predictive validity (e.g., future work with self-efficacy and autonomous learning) help support a scale's validity. Bandura suggested the use of factor analysis to determine item homogeneity (i.e., content validity) and Cronbach's alpha coefficient as a measure of internal consistency (i.e., reliability). A pilot test was performed on the original 21 items to determine a resultant instrument for the present study.

The first pilot group consisted of 77 participants selected (i.e., several convenience samples) from Regent University (n = 51) and Arkansas State University at Jonesboro (n = 26). With respect to the Regent University participants, some participants were staff members and not all student participants were from a given academic discipline (approximately 60% of the participants were students studying in the library and thus unknown to the researchers). All Arkansas State University participants were in-service teachers. The demographics of this pilot group are presented in Table 1 where the majority of the participants were female (P = 65%), White (P = 84%), and had a bachelor's degree (P = 56%). The average age of this pilot group was 34.96 years (SD = 12.13) and ranged from 21 to 63.

Descriptive statistics for each of the original 21 items is presented in Table 2. Because no item means are 100 (i.e., "certain can do"), it can be asserted that the ESS impediments represent obstacles within the context of adult autonomous learning. Because homogeneity of items is hypothesized to exist, principal component analysis was performed to uncover uncorrelated common factors that account for a maximum amount of variance in the subgroup of items (Dunteman, 1989) where the first principal component represents the best condensation of the variables (Gorsuch, 1983). However, because the principal component analysis was performed on the correlation matrix and because parsimony was desired, items of nonnormal character were identified for removal using the Kolmogorov-Smirnov Z (K-S Z) goodness-of-fit test. Because the score for each participant will be the summation of all items, the negative implications of committing a Type I error for each item's respective K-S Z test were assumed to be minimal; therefore, the K-S Z test of normality was based on α = 0.1. The results (see Table 2) suggest that items 1, 2, 4, 5, 7, 14, 15, 16, and 19 may be assumed to follow a normal distribution. The resultant 9-item ALA is presented in Appendix B.

Table 1. Pilot Group 1 ($N = 77$) Demographics

Variable	n
Gender	
Male	27
Female	50
Racial/Ethnic Group	
White	65
Black	7
Hispanic	2
Other	3
Highest Educational Attainment	
High School Diploma	14
Bachelor's Degree	43
Graduate Degree	20

Because principal component analysis was performed on the correlation matrix, results may be dependent upon sampling variability (Kim & Mueller, 1978). According to Kline (1993), a minimum subject-to-item ratio necessary for good factor analysis is 2:1 (p. 121) although he stated that there are large disagreements among researchers concerning this ratio. However, because the pilot group sample size to item number was approximately 9:1 (i.e., 77:9), the sample size was assumed to be sufficient for principal component analysis.

Table 2. Descriptive Statistics and Kolmogorov-Smirnov Z Test of the Original 21 Items for Pilot Group 1

Item	M	SD	Skewness	Kurtosis	K-S Z	p
1	62.16	24.01	-0.36	-0.43	0.997	0.274
2	66.14	24.96	-0.50	-0.62	0.994	0.277
3	81.94	18.71	-1.12	0.71	1.748	0.004*
4	66.56	24.55	-0.54	-0.45	1.017	0.252
5	58.56	25.64	-0.38	-0.44	0.885	0.413
6	74.69	20.50	-0.95	0.68	1.638	0.009*
7	58.51	26.77	-0.36	-0.61	1.173	0.127
8	65.55	25.55	-0.81	-0.04	1.462	0.028*
9	72.47	21.88	-0.80	0.20	1.258	0.084*
10	57.78	26.86	-0.47	-0.84	1.483	0.025*
11	57.22	32.43	-0.33	-1.17	1.288	0.073*
12	78.52	22.95	-1.23	0.87	1.738	0.005*
13	67.04	22.65	-0.76	0.06	1.500	0.022*
14	57.45	28.68	-0.53	-0.68	1.165	0.132
15	65.00	24.51	-0.77	0.08	1.222	0.101
16	68.05	23.97	-0.44	-0.61	1.163	0.134
17	72.99	25.73	-1.03	0.45	1.569	0.015*
18	80.78	21.21	-1.50	2.38	1.646	0.009*
19	64.35	24.98	-0.47	-0.46	1.203	0.111
20	77.99	22.28	-1.37	1.86	1.626	0.010*
21	68.68	23.67	-0.72	-0.21	1.422	0.031*

Note. Skewness $SE = 0.27$; kurtosis $SE = 0.54$. K-S Z refers to the Kolmogorov-Smirnov Z test with associated p-values.
*$p < 0.1$.

Table 3 presents the results of the principal component analysis performed on the nine items where normality was assumed. (Note that the item numbers in Table 3 correspond to the 21-item instrument presented in Appendix A and not the reduced 9-item instrument presented in Appendix B.) The Bartlett Test of Sphericity and the Kaiser-Meyer-Olkin Measure of Sampling Adequacy (MSA) were used to assess the suitability of the correlation matrix for factor analysis. For factor analysis, the MSA index should be greater than 0.5 (Cureton & D'Agostino, 1983, p. 389) and Bartlett's χ^2 should have a low p-value thereby enabling a rejection of the null hypothesis of no difference between the correlation matrix and the identity matrix (Norusis, 1988).

As presented in Table 3, MSA = 0.84 and Bartlett's $\chi^2(36, N = 77) =$ 322.98 with $p < 0.001$; thus, the pilot group sample was assumed adequate for principal component analysis. Gorsuch (1983) indicated that a minimum factor loading level of 0.3 (p. 210) is popularly used to define a salient loading. The results presented in Table 3 indicate that all nine items load above this criterion (minimum loading is 0.546) thereby supporting item homogeneity.

As suggested by Bandura (2001), Cronbach's alpha coefficient was computed to assess internal consistency. Kline (1993) suggested that alpha should be high at around 0.9 but not less than 0.7 (p. 11). Using the pilot group data, Cronbach's alpha was computed to equal 0.88 for the nine items associated with Table 3.

Based upon an analysis of the results of the pilot study, the ALA was reduced to nine items. These items were found to be homogeneous via principal component analysis and internally consistent via Cronbach's alpha coefficient thereby supporting content validity and internal reliability, respectively. The resultant items are presented in Appendix B and were used for a second pilot study.

Table 3. Principal Component Analysis of the Reduced 9-Item Instrument for Pilot Group 1

Item	Factor Loading
1	0.817
2	0.761
4	0.546
5	0.810
7	0.814
14	0.644
15	0.713
16	0.633
19	0.728

Note. Only one component extracted explaining 52.43% of the total variance. Kaiser-Meyer-Olkin Measure of Sampling Adequacy (MSA) = 0.84; Bartlett's Test of Sphericity approximate $\chi^2(36, N = 77) =$ 322.98, $p < 0.001$.

Second Pilot Study

A second pilot study was conducted using the 9-item version of the ALA. Fifty one graduate students attending Regent University participated in the second study. The purpose of this second study was to determine if the observed item homogeneity and internal consistency found in the first pilot study was present when the shortened ALA was used.

The 9-item ALA (Appendix B) was sent to all graduate students (approximately 500) attending programs in Regent University's School of Education (see Table 4). The majority of the second pilot group was female ($P = 80\%$), White ($P = 69\%$), and had a graduate degree ($P = 69\%$).

The descriptive statistics for the second pilot study are presented in Table 5. Note that item numbers 1 through 9 (Appendix B) correspond to item numbers 1, 2, 4, 5, 7, 14, 15, 16, and 19 (Appendix A), respectively. Comparing Table 5 to Table 2, the means for all nine items for pilot group 2 was larger than for pilot group 1. Because parsimony was not a goal of the second pilot study, item reduction via normality analysis was not performed.

Table 4. Pilot Group 2 ($N = 51$) Demographics

Variable	n
Gender	
Male	10
Female	41
Racial/Ethnic Group	
White	35
Black	13
Hispanic	1
Other	2
Highest Educational Attainment	
High School Diploma	0
Bachelor's Degree	16
Graduate Degree	35

Table 5. Descriptive Statistics for the 9-Item ALA from Pilot Group 2

Item	M	SD
1	70.35	21.76
2	76.27	18.70
3	72.37	19.83
4	72.67	20.21
5	67.74	21.66
6	65.39	24.37
7	79.31	18.52
8	75.96	20.79
9	71.18	22.13

The results of the principal component analysis are presented in Table 6. For this analysis, MSA = 0.76 and Bartlett's $\chi^2(36, N = 51) = 217.38$ with $p < 0.001$; thus, the second pilot group sample was assumed adequate for principal component analysis (Cureton & D'Agostino, 1983, p. 389; Norusis, 1988). According to the 0.3 criterion of Gorsuch (1983), all nine items have salient factor loadings; thus, items homogeneity is tenable. Cronbach's alpha coefficient was computed to equal 0.86 for the second pilot group; thus, internal consistency is supported as well.

Table 6. Principal Component Analysis of the 9-Item ALA for Pilot Group 2

Item	Factor Loading
1	0.707
2	0.734
3	0.656
4	0.797
5	0.775
6	0.623
7	0.765
8	0.490
9	0.718

Note. First component explaining 49.28% of the total variance. Kaiser-Meyer-Olkin Measure of Sampling Adequacy (MSA) = 0.76; Bartlett's Test of Sphericity approximate $\chi^2(36, N = 51) = 217.38, p < 0.001$.

Concluding Remarks

Based upon two pilot studies, the 9-item Appraisal of Learner Autonomy appears to be a valid and internally reliable instrument. Further research can now be undertaken in conjunction with the Learner Autonomy Profile to determine the tenability of the hypothesized causal relationship that self-efficacy mediates the influence of desire on the conative manifestations of resourcefulness, initiative, and persistence in autonomous learning. Support for this model will provide a greater level of understanding into methods of fostering learner autonomy via the sources of efficacy information.

The present investigation was performed as a logical next step in ongoing research to understand the psychological aspects of autonomous learning. Without adequate instrumentation, conjectures will not lead to tenable theories that support future empiricism into uncovering viable methods of empowering agents to further achievement. Self-efficacy has been argued to mediate all forms of cognitive motivation; thus, a research based understanding as to its role in autonomous learning is essential if we are to continue to move forward in developing lifelong learners.

Acknowledgements

The authors would like to thank Professor Albert Bandura (Stanford University) for his permission in using the Exercise Self-Efficacy Scale as the model for the Appraisal of Learner Autonomy.

References

Bandura, A. (1997). *Self-efficacy: The exercise of control.* New York, NY: W. H. Freeman and Company.

Bandura, A. (2001). *Guide for constructing self-efficacy scales.* Unpublished manuscript, Department of Psychology, Stanford University, Stanford, CA.

Bandura, A., & Locke, E. A. (2003). Negative self-efficacy and goal effects revisited. *Journal of Applied Psychology, 88*(1), 87-99.

Carr, P. B. (1999). *The measurement of resourcefulness intentions in the adult autonomous learner* (Unpublished doctoral dissertation). The George Washington University, Washington, DC.

Confessore, G. J. (1992). An introduction to the study of self-directed learning. In G. J. Confessore & S. J. Confessore (Eds.), *Guideposts to self-directed learning: Expert commentary on essential concepts* (pp. 1-6). King of Prussia, PA: Organization Design and Development.

Cureton, E. E., & D'Agostino, R. B. (1983). *Factor analysis: An applied approach.* Hillsdale, NJ: Lawrence Erlbaum Associates.

Darkenwald, G. G., & Valentine, T. (1985). Factor structure of deterrents to public participation in adult education. *Adult Education Quarterly, 35*(4), 177-193.

Derrick, M. G. (2001). *The measurement of an adult's intention to exhibit persistence in autonomous learning* (Unpublished doctoral dissertation). The George Washington University, Washington, DC.

Dunteman, G. H. (1989). *Principal components analysis.* Newbury Park, CA: SAGE.

Fishbein, M., & Ajzen, I. (1975). *Belief, attitude, intention, and behavior: An introduction to theory and research.* Reading, MA: Addison-Wesley.

Gorsuch, R. L. (1983). *Factor analysis.* Hillsdale, NJ: Lawrence Erlbaum Associates.

Hoban, G. J., & Sersland, C. J. (1998, February). *Developing learning plans for adult learners: Can self-efficacy predict a readiness for self-directed learning to determine effective modes of instruction?* Paper presented at the 12th International Symposium on Self-Directed Learning, Kissimmee, FL.

Kim, J., & Mueller, C. W. (1978). *Introduction to factor analysis: What it is and how to do it.* Beverly Hills, CA: SAGE.

Kline, P. (1993). *The handbook of psychological testing.* New York, NY: Routledge.

Meyer, D. T. (2001). *The measurement of intentional behavior as a prerequisite to autonomous learning* (Unpublished doctoral dissertation). The George Washington University, Washington, DC.

Norusis, M. J. (1988). *SPSS-X advanced statistics guide* (2nd ed.). Chicago, IL: SPSS.

Pajares, F., Hartley, J., & Valiante, G. (2001). Response format in writing self-efficacy assessment: Greater discrimination increases prediction. *Measurement & Evaluation in Counseling & Development, 33*(4), 214-221.

Park, E., & Confessore, G. J. (2002). Development of new instrumentation: Validation of the Learner Autonomy Profile beta version. In H. B. Long & Associates (Eds.), *Twenty-first century advances in self-directed learning* (pp. 289-306). Schaumburg, IL: Motorola University Press.

Ponton, M. K. (1999). *The measurement of an adult's intention to exhibit personal initiative in autonomous learning* (Unpublished doctoral dissertation). The George Washington University, Washington, DC.

Ponton, M. K., Carr, P. B., & Confessore, G. J. (2000). Learning conation: A psychological perspective of personal initiative and resourcefulness. In H. B. Long & Associates (Eds.), *Practice & theory in self-directed learning* (pp. 65-82). Schaumburg, IL: Motorola University Press.

Ponton, M. K., Carr, P. B., & Derrick, M. G. (2003, February). *A path analysis of the conative factors associated with autonomous learning.* Paper presented at the 17th International Self-Directed Learning Symposium, Cocoa Beach, FL. **[cf. Chapter 8]**

Ponton, M. K., Edmister, J. H., Ukeiley, L. S., & Seiner, J. M. (2001). Understanding the role of self-efficacy in engineering education. *Journal of Engineering Education, 90*(2), 247-251.

APPENDIX A

Appraisal of Learner Autonomy [Pilot Group Version]

In responding to the items below, insert any score (0-100) using the following scale:

0	10	20	30	40	50	60	70	80	90	100
Cannot do at all				Moderately certain can do						Certain can do

In each of the following situations, please rate how sure you are that you can get yourself to participate in a learning activity when nobody else requires you to do so. Note that a learning activity is <u>any</u> activity that you believe will help you to learn something that you want to learn.

(0-100)

1. When I am feeling tired _____

2. When I am feeling under pressure from work _____

3. During bad weather _____

4. After recovering from an injury that interrupted my learning _____

5. When I am experiencing personal problems _____

6. After I have experienced personal problems _____

7. When I am feeling depressed _____

8. When I am feeling anxious _____

9. After recovering from an illness that interrupted my learning _____

10. When I feel physical discomfort during my learning activity _____

11. During a vacation _____

12. After a vacation _____

13. When I have too much work to do at home   _____

14. When visitors are present   _____

15. When there are other interesting things to do   _____

16. When I am not getting near my learning goals   _____

17. Without support from my family   _____

18. Without support from my friends   _____

19. When I have other time commitments   _____

20. When I have a limited amount of money   _____

21. After experiencing family problems   _____

APPENDIX B

Appraisal of Learner Autonomy [Final Version]

In responding to the items below, insert any score (0-100) using the following scale:

0	10	20	30	40	50	60	70	80	90	100
Cannot do at all				Moderately certain can do						Certain can do

In each of the following situations, please rate how sure you are that you can get yourself to participate in a learning activity when nobody else requires you to do so. Note that a learning activity is <u>any</u> activity that you believe will help you to learn something that you want to learn.

(0-100)

1. When I am feeling tired   _____

2. When I am feeling under pressure from work   _____

3. After recovering from an injury that interrupted my learning _____

4. When I am experiencing personal problems   _____

5. When I am feeling depressed   _____

6. When visitors are present   _____

7. When there are other interesting things to do   _____

8. When I am not getting near my learning goals   _____

9. When I have other time commitments   _____

CHAPTER 13

THE LEARNER AUTONOMY PROFILE: A DISCUSSION OF SCALE COMBINATION TO MEASURE AUTONOMOUS LEARNING[13]

The Learner Autonomy Profile (LAP) was originally based upon four separate inventories developed to measure the following factors in an adult learner: desire, resourcefulness, initiative, and persistence. Although several studies have used scores for each of these scales and respective subscales in addressing proposed research questions, some recent studies have combined scale scores for subsequent analyses. The purpose of this chapter is to discuss the theoretical and statistical reasoning to support the usage of summative scores. Proposed is that a relevant measure of autonomous learning—as opposed to learner autonomy—would be to sum normalized measures of resourcefulness, initiative, and persistence. The current version of the LAP also includes a self-efficacy scale; however, limited data precludes inclusion in the presented analyses.

The Learner Autonomy Profile (LAP) was originally created as a combination of four separate inventories developed by Meyer (2001), Carr (1999), Ponton (1999), and Derrick (2001) to measure an adult learner's desire, resourcefulness, initiative, and persistence, respectively. The importance of these four constructs to personally satisfying learning endeavors was proposed by Confessore in 1992. Since its creation, the LAP has been used in numerous research projects (e.g., Derrick, Rovai, Ponton, Confessore, & Carr, 2007; Ponton, Derrick, & Carr, 2005) and dissertations (e.g., Berry, 2006; Flannagan, 2008; Liu, 2007; Palmer, 2003; Park, 2003; Wilson, 2004) that analyze these four scales (i.e., Inventory of Learner Desire, Inventory of Learner Resourcefulness, Inventory of Learner Initiative, and Inventory

---

[13]This article is reprinted with permission from the *International Journal for Self-Directed Learning* (http://sdlglobal.com/journals.php) and is copyrighted © The International Society for Self-Directed Learning [2008, *5*(1), 55-60]

of Learner Persistence), associated subscales, or relationships with other variables of hypothesized importance. On the contrary, some recent research has developed summative scores of all four scales (Derrick, Ponton, & Carr, 2005) or of select scales (Ponton, Derrick, Confessore, & Rhea, 2005). The purpose of this chapter is to discuss the theoretical and statistical reasoning behind an appropriate usage of summative scores. Note that individually the four inventories have been argued as being both construct and content valid as well as internally and externally reliable (Park & Confessore, 2002); therefore, the purpose of this chapter is not to analyze each inventory separately but rather to present an argument regarding scale combination. Since the LAP's creation, the Appraisal of Learner Autonomy (Ponton, Derrick, Hall, Rhea, & Carr, 2005) has been added to the battery to measure self-efficacy. To date, limited data have been used in research studies (Derrick, Ponton, Carr, Rovai, & Coe, 2007; Ponton, Derrick, Confessore, & Rhea, 2005); therefore, insufficient data exist to adequately support the analyses conducted for this chapter; a subsequent chapter will address the role of self-efficacy in learner autonomy.

Theoretical Framework

Ponton (1999) proposed a definition of *learner autonomy* as "the characteristic of the person who independently exhibits agency [i.e., intentional behavior] in learning activities" (pp. 13- 14). He argued that learner autonomy represents a subset of the cognitive and affective characteristics of the learner under a larger set associated with self-directedness. In contrast, Ponton suggested *autonomous learning* represents the conative manifestations of latent learner autonomy and is a subset of all agentic actions associated with a self-directed learning activity. Note that "conative" is used with autonomous learning because "conation refers to his [*sic*, i.e., the agent's] behavioral intentions" (Fishbein & Ajzen, 1975, p. 12) and subsequent intentional action.

The Inventory of Learner Desire (ILD) was developed by Meyer (2001) to assess an adult's ability to act intentionally (i.e., preconative factor). As Park and Confessore (2002) asserted, "[Meyer's] work on desire to learn has been treated as an effort to understand the *precursors* to the development of intentions related to learning" (p. 289). As a cognitive/affective scale, the ILD is argued as measuring a construct within the domain of learner autonomy, which is consistent with Ponton (1999).

The Inventories of Learner Resourcefulness (ILR; Carr, 1999), Initiative (ILI; Ponton, 1999), and Persistence (ILP; Derrick, 2001) measure learner intentions with respect to learning activities. As such, these scales explicitly focus on conation; a domain that Ponton (1999) theorized to be relevant to autonomous learning. Based upon the theoretical arguments of learner autonomy vis-à-vis autonomous learning where the former is cognitive/affective and the latter is conative/behavioral, hypothesized is that combining ILR, ILI, and ILP scores to generate an aggregate autonomous learning score is conceptually tenable. The ILD should be used to help assess learner autonomy perhaps in concert with other measures in the cognitive/affective domains (e.g., self-efficacy, motivation). Expected are relevant correlation analyses (e.g., intercorrelations, principal component analysis, and Cronbach's alpha) to support this grouping.

Findings

The data from a nonprobability sample of 2,277 adults were analyzed. These data represent samples from various research studies using the LAP. The average age of the participants was 33.0 years ($SD = 11.5$) and ranged from 16 to 88 years. The majority were female ($n = 1,486$; $P = 65.3\%$) and the level of education was as follows: high school diploma/G.E.D., $n = 1,008$; bachelor's degree, $n = 534$; graduate/professional degree, $n = 735$.

Table 1 presents the intercorrelations between the four scales. Whereas all correlations are significant at the .01 level (2-tailed), the ILD moderately correlates with the ILR, ILI, and ILP while these last three scales correlate highly with each other ("moderate" and "high" as defined by Hinkle, Wiersma, & Jurs, 1998, p. 120). These results suggest a stronger linear relationship between the autonomous learning scales (i.e., ILR, ILI, and ILP) as compared to ILD paired correlations.

Table 1. Intercorrelations Between Scales ($N = 2,277$)

Scale	1	2	3	4
1. ILD	-	.617*	.591*	.601*
2. ILR		-	.862*	.849*
3. ILI			-	.881*
4. ILP				-

*$p < .01$ (2-tailed)

Table 2 presents the factor loadings using exploratory, unrotated principal component analysis (PCA) performed on the correlation matrix; Kaiser-Meyer-Olkin Measure of Sampling Adequacy = .84; Bartlett's Test of Sphericity approximate $\chi^2(6, N = 2,277) = 8,004.9$, $p < .001$. Gorsuch (1983) stated the first principal component represents the best condensation of a group of variables; thus, because the ILD, ILR, ILI, and ILP are linked to related theoretical constructs (i.e., learner autonomy and autonomous learning), it should be no surprise that the loadings are high and in the first component (Gorsuch asserted a minimum salient loading to be 0.3, p. 210). However, note that the highest loadings are for the ILR, ILI, and ILP scales.

The intercorrelation and PCA results suggest that the theorized grouping of ILR, ILI, and ILP scales may be tenable. Thus, a confirmatory PCA was performed on the correlation matrix for a 2-factor solution using Varimax rotation with Kaiser Normalization (2 factors were chosen to correspond to the constructs of learner autonomy and autonomous learning). As is evident in Table 3, the loadings for the ILR, ILI, and ILP are high for the first component (i.e., autonomous learning) whereas the ILD loading is singularly high for the second component (i.e., learner autonomy).

Table 4 presents the reliability statistics using Cronbach's alpha coefficient for internal consistency. The findings indicate that only by removing ILD scores will Cronbach's alpha increase above the value computed using all four scales.

Table 2. Exploratory Principal Component Analysis

Scale	Loading
ILD	.764
ILR	.936
ILI	.939
ILP	.937

Note. Only one component extracted explaining 80.5% of the total variance.

Table 3. Confirmatory 2-Factor Principal Component Analysis

Scale	Loading	
	Component 1	Component 2
ILD	.335	.942
ILR	.879	.349
ILI	.913	.299
ILP	.901	.316

Note. Component 1 explaining 63.3% of the total variance; Components 1 and 2 explaining 93.2%.

Table 4. Reliability Statistics

Scale	Cronbach's Alpha if Item Deleted
ILD	.949
ILR	.872
ILI	.870
ILP	.871

Note. Cronbach's alpha using all 4 items: .918.

Concluding Remarks

The combination of scales is a theoretical argument based upon the constructs of under analysis. In this regard, it makes conceptual sense to group the Inventories of Learner Resourcefulness, Initiative, and Persistence together as they are theorized to exist within the conative/behavioral domain of *autonomous learning*; alternatively, the Inventory of Learner Desire exists within the cognitive/affective domain of *learner autonomy*. Confirmatory principal component analysis supports this grouping of scales. The results presented were based upon correlations and, as such, are independent of linear transformations of variables. However, the number of items associated with the ILR, ILI, and ILP are 53, 44, and 34, respectively. Therefore, if a proposed analysis were to be based on total score, it would be important to normalize each inventory before combining thereby avoiding an uneven weighting of scales in the summation. As correlations are not affected by this linear transformation, correlation based analyses between scales could still be performed on the normalized data.

References

Berry, C. A. (2006). *The assessment of learner autonomy and persistence in adults enrolled in online courses* (Unpublished doctoral dissertation). Regent University, Virginia Beach, VA.

Carr, P. B. (1999). *The measurement of resourcefulness intentions in the adult autonomous learner* (Unpublished doctoral dissertation). The George Washington University, Washington, DC.

Confessore, G. J. (1992). An introduction to the study of self-directed learning. In G. J. Confessore & S. J. Confessore (Eds.), *Guideposts to self-directed learning: Expert commentary on essential concepts* (pp. 1-6). King of Prussia, PA: Organization Design and Development.

Derrick, M. G. (2001). *The measurement of an adult's intention to exhibit persistence in autonomous learning* (Unpublished doctoral dissertation). The George Washington University, Washington, DC.

Derrick, M. G., Ponton, M. K., & Carr, P. B. (2005). A preliminary analysis of learner autonomy in online and face-to-face settings. *International Journal of Self-Directed Learning, 2*(1), 62-70.

Derrick, M. G., Ponton, M. K., Carr, P. B., Rovai, A. P., & Coe, J. G. (2007, January). *Review of the finding on the relationship of curiosity and autonomous learning.* Paper presented at the 21st International Self-Directed Learning Symposium, Cocoa Beach, FL.

Derrick, M. G., Rovai, A. P., Ponton, M. K., Confessore, G. J., & Carr, P. B. (2007). An examination of the relationship of gender, marital status, and prior educational attainment and learner autonomy. *Educational Research and Review, 2*(1), 1-8.

Fishbein, M., & Ajzen, I. (1975). *Belief, attitude, intention, and behavior: An introduction to theory and research.* Reading, MA: Addison-Wesley.

Flannagan, J. S. (2008). *A study of student achievement based on autonomous learning and self-efficacy* (Unpublished doctoral dissertation). Regent University, Virginia Beach, VA.

Gorsuch, R. L. (1983). *Factor analysis.* Hillsdale, NJ: Lawrence Erlbaum Associates.

Hinkle, D. E., Wiersma, W., & Jurs, S. G. (1998). *Applied statistics for the behavioral sciences* (4th ed.). Boston, MA: Houghton Mifflin.

Liu, J. (2007). *Learner autonomy and Chinese university students' English proficiency: A quantitative and qualitative study* (Unpublished doctoral dissertation). Regent University, Virginia Beach, VA.

Meyer, D. T. (2001). *The measurement of intentional behavior as a prerequisite to autonomous learning* (Unpublished doctoral dissertation). The George Washington University, Washington, DC.

Palmer, C. A. (2003). *Linking learner autonomy and conditions for learning in the workplace: Knowledge management systems as organizing circumstances* (Unpublished doctoral dissertation). The George Washington University, Washington, DC.

Park, E. (2003). *Learner autonomy in selected populations of East Asian graduate students who study at institutions in the United States* (Unpublished doctoral dissertation). The George Washington University, Washington, DC.

Park, E., & Confessore, G. J. (2002). Development of new instrumentation: Validation of the Learner Autonomy Profile beta version. In H. B. Long & Associates (Eds.), *Twenty first century advances in self-directed learning* (pp. 289-306). Schaumburg, IL: Motorola University Press.

Ponton, M. K. (1999). *The measurement of an adult's intention to exhibit personal initiative in autonomous learning* (Unpublished doctoral dissertation). The George Washington University, Washington, DC.

Ponton, M. K., Derrick, M. G., & Carr, P. B. (2005). The relationship between resourcefulness and persistence in adult autonomous learning. *Adult Education Quarterly, 55*(2), 116-128. **[cf. Chapter 9]**

Ponton, M. K., Derrick, M. G., Confessore, G. J., & Rhea, N. E. (2005). The role of self-efficacy in autonomous learning. *International Journal of Self-Directed Learning, 2*(2), 81-90. **[cf. Chapter 10]**

Ponton, M. K., Derrick, M. G., Hall, J. M., Rhea, N. E., & Carr, P. B. (2005). The relationship between self-efficacy and autonomous learning: The development of new instrumentation. *International Journal of Self-Directed Learning*, 2(1), 50-61. **[cf. Chapter 12]**

Wilson, D. M. (2004). *The correlation between racial identity development and learner autonomy of African-American students* (Unpublished doctoral dissertation). The George Washington University, Washington, DC.

CHAPTER 14

SELF-EFFICACY AND THE LEARNER AUTONOMY PROFILE[14]

In 2004, the Appraisal of Learner Autonomy (ALA) was created as a measure of self-efficacy in autonomous learning. Since 2005, it has been offered in conjunction with the Learner Autonomy Profile (LAP) and has been completed by over 2,000 subjects. The purpose of this chapter is to present recent analyses to better articulate the usefulness of the ALA within the context of the LAP and to discuss related implications to the study of adult learning. The findings suggest that the ALA offers important explanatory utility in understanding learner autonomy and predicting autonomous learning.

The Learner Autonomy Profile (LAP; licensed to Human Resource Development Enterprises, HRDE) was initially developed as a battery of four instruments: the Inventory of Learner Desire (ILD; cf. Meyer, 2001), the Inventory of Learner Resourcefulness (ILR; cf. Carr, 1999), the Inventory of Learner Initiative (ILI; cf. Ponton, 1999), and the Inventory of Learner Persistence (ILP; cf. Derrick, 2001). The purpose of the LAP is to use these measures of the four conative factors of desire, resourcefulness, initiative, and persistence (cf. Confessore, 1992) as a method of determining the extent to which an adult tends to engage in agentic learning, which is a defining characteristic of autonomous learning (Ponton, 1999, 2009). To this end, HRDE continued instrument refinement (Park & Confessore, 2002) and currently engages in the coaching of those adults around the world who are interested in increasing their learner autonomy.

In 2004, Ponton, Derrick, Carr, and Hall presented the Appraisal of Learner Autonomy (ALA) as a measure of self-efficacy in autonomous learning. The construct of self-efficacy has been supported empirically as an important mediator between motivation and agency (Bandura,

---

[14]This article is reprinted with permission from the *International Journal for Self-Directed Learning* (http://sdlglobal.com/journals.php) and is copyrighted © The International Society for Self-Directed Learning [2010, 7(2), 54-63]

1997); therefore, Ponton et al. (2004) argued that such a measure was essential in furthering the understanding of learner autonomy. The 9-item final version of the ALA (Ponton, Derrick, Hall, Rhea, & Carr, 2005) was argued as valid and has been used as part of the LAP since its publication in 2005 (note that the ALA is unlicensed and is available for research in its entirety in Ponton, Derrick, Hall, et al., 2005, as well as in Chapter 12 in this compendium). At this time, over 2,000 people have taken the ALA in conjunction with the administration of the LAP by HRDE.

Ponton (1999) offered a definition of learner autonomy as "the characteristic of the person who independently exhibits agency [i.e., intentional behavior] in learning activities" (pp. 13-14). He argued that the construct of *learner autonomy* exists within the cognitive/affective domains of the learner and that *autonomous learning* represents the resultant conative manifestations (i.e., intentional action) of such latent autonomy. The ILD was conceptualized as a preconative measure of the degree to which a person can act intentionally in any domain of functioning (cf. Meyer, 2001, Inventory of Intentional Behavior) whereas the ILR (Carr, 1999), ILI (Ponton, 1999), and ILP (Derrick, 2001) were designed as conative measures within the domain of adult learning. Self-efficacy is a belief of personal capability to engage successfully in a given performance (Bandura, 1997); therefore, the ALA—a measure of one's belief in requisite ability to successfully engage in autonomous learning—exists within the preconative domain similar to the ILD.

There has been potential ambiguity in the literature with respect to whether conative constructs should be included in the learner autonomy or autonomous learning domains (cf. Ponton, Derrick, Confessore, & Rhea, 2005; Ponton & Schuette, 2008). Ponton, Derrick, Confessore, et al. (2005) stated the following:

> It should be noted that *showing* resourcefulness, initiative, and persistence in one's learning is conceptually separable from what is measured . . . [by the ILR, ILI, and ILP]. The ILR, ILI, and ILP are measures of *intention to show* resourcefulness, initiative, and persistence. These instruments were developed in this manner because it is not possible to know, a priori, whether or not study participants are currently engaged in autonomous learning activities (cf. Ponton, 1999). Further research is necessary to

uncover the strength of the relationship between the intention to engage in autonomous learning and the enactment of the behaviors of autonomous learning, the latter being the exhibition of resourcefulness, initiative, and persistence. (p. 86)

Thus, autonomous learning represents the actual manifestation of action related constructs (e.g., resourcefulness, initiative, and persistence) and not merely an intention to manifest such action. Using the conative measures of the ILR, ILI, and ILP to characterize autonomous learning as was done in Ponton and Schuette (2008) *is by proxy only* as there does not exist any way of knowing whether or not a randomly selected study participant is currently engaged in an autonomous learning activity for a direct measure of autonomous learning to be applied. In addition, as the present conative constructs are cognitively based (e.g., anticipating the future benefits of learning as part of the ILR), such direct measures cannot be limited to behavioral observations but rather must encompass a constellation of measures associated with self-reported "action-related concepts" (Chapman & Skinner, 1985, p. 201) under the larger umbrella of action theory.

To test this conceptual differentiation between learner autonomy and autonomous learning, Ponton and Schuette (2008) conducted a 2-factor confirmatory principal component analysis (PCA) using ILD, ILR, ILI, and ILP data from a nonprobability sample of 2,277 adults; insufficient ALA data precluded an inclusion of this measure in the analysis at that time. The PCA results supported the hypothesized separation of learner autonomy—represented by ILD measurements—and autonomous learning as represented by proxy by the ILR, ILI, and ILP measurements. Based on these results, they proposed it would be tenable to combine ILR, ILI, and ILP scores as a singular measure of *autonomous learning* (i.e., a new variable) provided each measure were normalized by the number of items in its respective scale (it could certainly be argued that normalization is required at the subscale level as well; however, this argument has not been investigated to date).

The continued use of the ALA in conjunction with the LAP has resulted in a data set of sufficient size to continue this analysis; Comrey and Lee (as cited in Tabachnick & Fidell, 2007, p. 613) stated that a sample size of 1,000 is excellent for factor analysis. Note that there is no necessary reason to continue to define autonomous learning via proxy measure arguments in order to make comparisons to learner autonomy constructs; theoretically, preconative and conative constructs should be separable as well. Thus, it is hypothesized that a 2-factor confirmatory PCA would support the separation of the ALA and ILD vis-à-vis the ILR, ILI, and ILP based upon the conceptual separation of the preconative and conative domains of learner autonomy. The purpose of this investigation is to test this research hypothesis. Furthering our understanding of the relationship between these measures will help us to continue to assess the appropriateness of making causal arguments for facilitating autonomous learning using Fishbein and Ajzen's (1975) behavioral model that relates cognition, affection, and conation to intentional behavior. Based on this continued understanding, future studies would require the use of structural equation modeling to test directional relationships.

Method

The data from a nonprobability sample of 2,074 adults were analyzed. These data represent a conglomeration of samples from numerous research studies in which both the LAP and ALA were administered. The average age of the participants in this resultant sample was 28.1 years ($SD = 12.0$). The majority were female ($n = 1,496$; $P = 72.1\%$) and the level of education was as follows: high school diploma/G.E.D., $n = 1,205$, $P = 58.1\%$; bachelor's degree, $n = 324$, $P = 15.6\%$; and graduate/professional degree, $n = 518$, $P = 25.0\%$ (note that 27 participants, $P = 1.3\%$, did not respond to this field).

Findings

Table 1 presents the intercorrelations between the five scales. All correlations are significant at the .01 level (2-tailed), and the ILD moderately correlates with the ILR, ILI, and ILP whereas these last three scales correlate highly with each other. The ALA moderately correlates with the ILR, ILI, and ILP, and its correlation with the ILD is low. ("Low," "moderate," and "high" correlation descriptions as per Hinkle, Wiersma, & Jurs, 1998, p. 120, for correlation ranges .30 to .50, .50 to .70, and .70 to .90, respectively.) Internal consistency for each scale is reflected in the following Cronbach alpha coefficients: ILD, .93; ILR, .96; ILI, .97; ILP, .97; and ALA, .89.

Table 1. Intercorrelations Between Scales ($N = 2{,}074$)

Scale	1	2	3	4	5
1. ILD	-	.573*	.521*	.549*	.391*
2. ILR		-	.843*	.854*	.552*
3. ILI			-	.893*	.592*
4. ILP				-	.577*
5. ALA					-

*$p < .01$ (2-tailed)

Inspection of histograms (not presented) suggests normality for all five measures with each distribution having a slight negative skewness. Linearity is supported by the product-moment correlations presented in Table 1; as PCA was performed as opposed to factor analysis, multicollinearity is not a concern (no matrix inversion in PCA; Tabachnick & Fidell, 2007).

Table 2 presents the factor loadings using exploratory, unrotated PCA performed on the correlation matrix. Compared to factor analysis, PCA is the preferred method of factor extraction for exploratory studies (Mertler & Vannatta, 2005, p. 250); thus, it was used in this investigation for the purpose of data reduction where it is presumed that the principal components are based upon the measured responses (DeCoster, 1998). The sole purpose of performing this preliminary analysis was to determine if there was any initial indication that the five scales were statistically unrelated, which would be in contrast to their theoretical classification as salient aspects of learner autonomy. The Kaiser-Meyer-Olkin Measure of Sampling Adequacy (MSA) and the Bartlett Test of Sphericity were used to assess the suitability of the correlation matrix for factor analysis. For factor analysis, the MSA index should be no less than 0.5 (Cureton & D'Agostino, 1983, p. 389). In addition, Bartlett's χ^2 should enable a rejection of the null hypothesis of no difference between the correlation matrix and the identity matrix (i.e., common factors cannot exist unless partial correlations between items exist; Norusis, 1988) although this test is likely to be statistically significant for large sample sizes even with low correlations (Tabachnick & Fidell, 2007). The resultant MSA = .86 and Bartlett's Test of Sphericity approximate $\chi^2(10, N = 2074) = 8{,}102.1, p < .001$, suggest the sample was adequate for PCA. Gorsuch (1983) stated the first principal component represents the best condensation of a group of variables; thus, because the ILD, ILR, ILI, ILP, and ALA are linked to a related theoretical construct (i.e., learner autonomy), it should be no surprise that the loadings are high (Gorsuch asserted a minimum salient loading to be 0.3, p. 210, which is consistent with Tabachnick & Fidell's suggestion to only interpret variables with loadings of 0.32 or greater, p. 649) in the first component. Note that the highest loadings—all greater than 0.9—are for the ILR, ILI, and ILP scales.

Table 2. Exploratory Principal Component Analysis: All Scales

Scale	Loading
ILD	.698
ILR	.920
ILI	.928
ILP	.933
ALA	.722

Note. Only one component extracted explaining 71.7% of the total variance.

The intercorrelation and PCA results suggest that the hypothesized grouping of ILR, ILI, and ILP scales versus a grouping of ILD and ALA may be testable using linear methods. Thus, a confirmatory PCA was performed on the correlation matrix for a 2-factor solution using Oblimin rotation with Kaiser normalization (2 factors were chosen to correspond to the preconative and conative constructs of learner autonomy). Note that oblique rotation was chosen because it would be reasonable to expect that preconative and conative aspects of learner autonomy would correlate—conation results from beliefs as per Fishbein and Ajzen (1975)—thus making oblique rotation tenable. The resultant correlation between the two components is 0.44 (see Table 3), which is greater than the 0.32 minimum recommended by Tabachnick and Fidell (2007, p. 646) as justifying oblique rotation. As is evident in Table 3, the loadings for the ILR, ILI, ILP, and ALA are highest for the first component whereas the ILD loading is highest for the second component; cross loadings do not suggest a more complex interpretation than this separation. This is in contrast to the hypothesized 2-factor solution separating preconation as represented by the ILD and ALA versus conation as represented by the ILR, ILI, and ILP.

Table 3. Pattern Matrix for Confirmatory 2-Factor PCA: All Scales

Scale	Loading	
	Component 1	Component 2
ILD	.097	.902
ILR	.747	.302
ILI	.840	.182
ILP	.807	.236
ALA	.922	-.242

Note. Extraction sums of squared loadings: (a) For Component 1, 3.587 (71.7% of the total variance); for Component 2, .617 (12.3% of the total variance). Rotation (Oblimin with Kaiser normalization) sums of squared loadings: (a) For Component 1, 3.352; for Component 2, 1.955. Correlation between Components 1 and 2: $r = .44$.

Because the ILR, ILI, ILP, and ALA constituted the first principal component, a hierarchical regression analysis was performed to determine the predictive utility of the ALA on conation. Note that a new variable *conative learner autonomy* was created by summing ILR, ILI, and ILP scores where each is normalized by its respective number of items (i.e., 53, 44, and 34, respectively; cf. Ponton & Schuette, 2008). The ALA was chosen as the baseline model (i.e., Step 1a; see Table 4), and because of the statistically significant correlation between the ILD and the other four scales, the ILD was added to the ALA in Step 2. Both Step 1a and Step 2 models are significant at the .001 level; $F(1, 2072) = 1179.1$ and $F(2, 2071) = 1025.2$, respectively. The change in R^2 from Step 1a to 2 (i.e., .135) is also significant at the .001 level.

If the ILD were chosen as the independent variable for *conative learner autonomy* in a second baseline model (i.e., Step 1b; see Table 4), the model is also significant, $F(1, 2072) = 1016.2$, $p < .001$, with $R^2 = .329$ versus .363 when using the ALA as the independent variable. As would be expected, the change in R^2 by adding the ALA as a second independent variable to this new baseline model (i.e., .169) is also significant at the .001 level. Thus, the ALA is a slightly stronger predictor for *conative learner autonomy* when compared to the ILD due to an increase of 3.4% (i.e., .363 - .329) in explained variance.

Table 4. Summary of Hierarchical Regression Analysis for Variables
Predicting Conative Learner Autonomy (ILR_{norm} + ILI_{norm} + ILP_{norm})

Variable	B	SE B	β
Step 1a			
ALA	.015	.000	.602**
Step 1b			
ILD	.057	.002	.574**
Step 2			
ALA	.011	.000	.446**
ILD	.040	.002	.399**

Note. R^2 = .363 for Step 1a; R^2 = .329 for Step 1b; R^2 = .498 for Step 2
($p < .001$ for change from either Step 1a or 1b).
**$p < .001$.

Focusing on the ILR, ILI, ILP, and ALA and following the hypothesized separation of preconation (i.e., ALA) and conation (i.e., ILR, ILI, and ILP), a confirmatory PCA was performed on the correlation matrix for a 2-factor solution using Oblimin rotation with Kaiser normalization for the ILD, ILR, ILI, and ALA. MSA = .83 and Bartlett's Test of Sphericity approximate $\chi^2(6, N = 2,074) = 7,224.0$, $p < .001$; thus, the sample was deemed adequate for PCA using this reduced variable set. In addition, the correlation between components is 0.60 (see Table 5) thereby supporting oblique rotation. As is evident in Table 5, the loadings for the ILR, ILI, and ILP are highest for the first component whereas the ALA loading is highest for the second component; cross loadings do not suggest a more complex interpretation than this separation.

Table 5. Pattern Matrix for Confirmatory 2-Factor PCA: ILD Scale
Excluded

| Scale | Loading | |
	Component 1	Component 2
ILR	.962	-.031
ILI	.934	.036
ILP	.960	.001
ALA	.001	.999

Note. Extraction sums of squared loadings: (a) For Component 1, 3.181
(79.5% of the total variance); for Component 2, .548 (13.7% of the
total variance). Rotation (Oblimin with Kaiser normalization) sums of
squared loadings: (a) For Component 1, 3.088; for Component 2,
1.986. Correlation between Components 1 and 2: $r = .60$.

Discussion

The research hypothesis is not supported by the findings; that is, the
expected separation of the ILD and ALA (within the preconative
domain of learner autonomy) versus the ILR, ILI, and ILP (within the
conative domain of learner autonomy) is not tenable (see Table 3). The
factor loadings associated with the ILR, ILI, ILP, and ALA on the first
principal component suggest a common latent construct among these
measures.

Meyer (2001) created an instrument that assesses the degree to
which an adult can act intentionally based upon three constituent
subscales: basic freedoms, managing power, and acquired skills. From
her original instrument titled the Inventory of Intentional Behavior, the
ILD evolved; however, the ILD does not actually represent a measure
within the context of learning but rather represents a measure of
theoretical importance to any agentic action of which autonomous
learning is but one example. As Park and Confessore (2002) stated,
"[Meyer's] work on desire to learn has been treated as an effort to
understand the *precursors* to the development of intentions related to
learning" (p. 289).

In contrast to the ILD, the ILR, ILI, ILP, and ALA are
contextualized to learning. Carr's (1999) ILR assesses the degree to
which an adult (a) anticipates the future benefits of learning, (b)
prioritizes learning over nonlearning activities, (c) chooses to engage in
learning versus nonlearning activities, and (d) solves problems that

impede desired learning. Ponton's (1999) ILI assesses the following behavioral intentions in an adult learner as manifest with respect to a learning activity: goal-directedness, action-orientation, persistence in overcoming obstacles, active-approach to problem solving, and self-startedness. Derrick's (2001) ILP measures the sustained maintenance of the following behaviors in learning: volition, self-regulation, and goal-directedness. Finally, the ALA (Ponton, Derrick, Hall, et al., 2005) measures the perceived capability of an adult to engage in autonomous learning in the face of impediments to personal agency.

In the PCA model, "the principal components are based on the measured responses" (DeCoster, 1998, p. 3); thus, the interpretation of the results presented in Table 3 is that the first principal component is associated with learner autonomy based on beliefs of efficacy and intentions to exhibit resourcefulness, initiative, and persistence within the context of learning. The ILR, ILI, ILP, and ALA are all contextualized to adult learning and have been argued as together supporting autonomous learning; however, the ILD is not contextualized to learning. Therefore, the PCA results may have separated the five variables along the dimension of learning, which appears theoretically possible. When this dimension is controlled (i.e., when the ILD is removed from the PCA; see Table 5), factor loadings again support the theoretical separation of preconative learner autonomy (related to the ALA) and conative learner autonomy (related to the ILR, ILI, and ILP).

The present results suggest that the reason asserted by Ponton and Schuette (2008) for the separation of the ILD vis-à-vis the ILR, ILI, and ILP may not be the relationship between preconation and conation but rather is a result of the varied contextualization to learning; however, this could not have been assessed in 2008 without the ALA data. Controlling for learning contextualization results in a component structure that still supports the conclusion of Ponton and Schuette (2008) regarding the appropriateness for summing normalized ILR, ILI, and ILP scores into a new variable existing within the conative domain of learner autonomy versus the preconative domain of learner autonomy as represented in part by the ALA.

The separate, predictive utility of either the ALA or the ILD on a new variable *conative learner autonomy* is statistically significant at the .001 level and qualitatively similar: $R^2 = .363$ for the ALA versus .329 for the ILD. In addition, using both as independent variables, the total variance explained in *conative learner autonomy* is 49.8% (see Table 4), which compares reasonably to the 59.7% previously reported by

Ponton, Derrick, Confessore, et al. (2005) in their preliminary study of 82 adults using the same independent variables but rather a summation of nonnormalized ILR, ILI, and ILP scores for a reduced variable. Note that the addition of either the ALA or the ILD to the model results in a statistically significant increase in R^2 at the .001 level; thus, the model is more fully specified when both scales are included. The low correlation between the ILD and ALA (see Table 1) suggests that each accounts for separate variance in *conative learner autonomy* although the 49.8% of variance explained suggests that there are still more preconative measures (e.g., motivation, personal responsibility) required to fully specify a prediction model.

The degree to which a person believes himself or herself generally capable of acting as an agent, which is assessed by the ILD, will manifest itself in the intentional activities, or lack thereof, of the agent. The statistical findings associated with the ILD, ILR, ILI, and ILP are consistent in numerous studies over several years in that the ILD has always exhibited a statistically significant and moderate to high correlation with the other three measures either separately or in summation; thus, the degree of extant agency is well established as being related to the degree to which an adult intends to engage in autonomous learning. It is interesting, however, that the ALA does exhibit some interesting statistical properties when compared to the ILD: (a) it loads with the ILR, ILI, and ILP along the proposed dimension of learner autonomy; (b) it loads separately from the ILR, ILI, and ILP when the dimension of learning is controlled along the argued dimensions of preconation versus conation; and (c) it accounts for more variance (albeit slightly) with respect to the reduced variable *conative learner autonomy*. However, the regression model associated with the criterion variable *conative learner autonomy* is more fully specified when both the ILD and ALA are included as independent variables.

Thus, it is asserted that the ALA offers some important explanatory utility in understanding learner autonomy and predicting autonomous learning. Specifically, in support of HRDE's coaching interests, the ALA should be offered as part of the LAP and inform resultant interventions that promote learner autonomy using the sources of efficacy information outlined by Bandura (1997): mastery experiences, verbal persuasion, vicarious experiences, and interpretations of physiological/emotive arousals. Generally, as we continue to further our understanding of adult learning, the ALA should be used in conjunction with other studies to continue to define and inform the causal role of self-efficacy in agentic learning.

References

Bandura, A. (1997). *Self-efficacy: The exercise of control.* New York, NY: W. H. Freeman and Company.

Carr, P. B. (1999). *The measurement of resourcefulness intentions in the adult autonomous learner* (Unpublished doctoral dissertation). The George Washington University, Washington, DC.

Chapman, M., & Skinner, E. A. (1985). Action in development— Development in action. In M. Frese & J. Sabini (Eds.), *Goal-directed behavior: The concept of action in psychology* (pp. 200-213). Hillsdale, NJ: Lawrence Erlbaum Associates.

Confessore, G. J. (1992). An introduction to the study of self-directed learning. In G. J. Confessore & S. J. Confessore (Eds.), *Guideposts to self-directed learning: Expert commentary on essential concepts* (pp. 1-6). King of Prussia, PA: Organization Design and Development.

Cureton, E. E., & D'Agostino, R. B. (1983). *Factor analysis: An applied approach.* Hillsdale, NJ: Lawrence Erlbaum Associates.

DeCoster, J. (1998). *Overview of factor analysis.* Retrieved from http://www.stat-help.com/factor.pdf

Derrick, M. G. (2001). *The measurement of an adult's intention to exhibit persistence in autonomous learning* (Unpublished doctoral dissertation). The George Washington University, Washington, DC.

Fishbein, M., & Ajzen, I. (1975). *Belief, attitude, intention, and behavior: An introduction to theory and research.* Reading, MA: Addison-Wesley.

Gorsuch, R. L. (1983). *Factor analysis.* Hillsdale, NJ: Lawrence Erlbaum Associates.

Hinkle, D. E., Wiersma, W., & Jurs, S. G. (1998). *Applied statistics for the behavioral sciences* (4th ed.). Boston, MA: Houghton Mifflin.

Mertler, C. A., & Vannatta, R. A. (2005). *Advanced and multivariate statistical methods: Practical application and interpretation* (3rd ed.). Glendale, CA: Pyrczak.

Meyer, D. T. (2001). *The measurement of intentional behavior as a prerequisite to autonomous learning* (Unpublished doctoral dissertation). The George Washington University, Washington, DC.

Norusis, M. J. (1988). *SPSS-X advanced statistics guide* (2nd ed.). Chicago, IL: SPSS.

Park, E., & Confessore, G. J. (2002). Development of new instrumentation: Validation of the Learner Autonomy Profile beta version. In H. B. Long & Associates (Eds.), *Twenty-first century advances in self-directed learning* (pp. 289-306). Schaumburg, IL: Motorola University Press.

Ponton, M. K. (1999). *The measurement of an adult's intention to exhibit personal initiative in autonomous learning* (Unpublished doctoral dissertation). The George Washington University, Washington, DC.

Ponton, M. K. (2009). An agentic perspective contrasting autonomous learning with self-directed learning. In M. G. Derrick & M. K. Ponton (Eds.), *Emerging directions in self-directed learning* (pp. 65-76). Chicago, IL: Discovery Association Publishing House. [cf. **Chapter 4**]

Ponton, M. K., Derrick, M. G., Carr, P. B., & Hall, J. M. (2004, February). *The relationship between self-efficacy and autonomous learning.* Paper presented at the 18th International Self-Directed Learning Symposium, Cocoa Beach, FL. [cf. **Chapter 12**]

Ponton, M. K., Derrick, M. G., Confessore, G. J., & Rhea, N. E. (2005). The role of self-efficacy in autonomous learning. *International Journal of Self-Directed Learning, 2*(2), 81-90. [cf. **Chapter 10**]

Ponton, M. K., Derrick, M. G., Hall, J. M., Rhea, N. E., & Carr, P. B. (2005). The relationship between self-efficacy and autonomous learning: The development of new instrumentation. *International Journal of Self-Directed Learning, 2*(1), 50-61. [cf. **Chapter 12**]

Ponton, M. K., & Schuette, C. T. (2008). The Learner Autonomy Profile: A discussion of scale combination to measure autonomous learning. *International Journal of Self-Directed Learning, 5*(1), 55-60. [cf. **Chapter 13**]

Tabachnick, B. G., & Fidell, L. S. (2007). *Using multivariate statistics* (5th ed.). Boston, MA: Pearson Education.

Printed in the USA
CPSIA information can be obtained
at www.ICGtesting.com
CBHW052254151024
15933CB00024B/531